Preventing Internal Theft

A Bar Owner's Guide
Second Edition

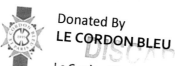
Robert Plotkin
Copyright 1998 BarMedia

OTHER BOOKS BY ROBERT PLOTKIN

Drinks for All Ages: The Original Guide to Alcohol-Free Beverages and Drinks (2002)
The Professional Bartender's Training Manual — 3rd Edition (2002)
¡Toma! Margaritas! The Original Guide to Margaritas and Tequila (Revised - 2002)
The Bartender's Companion — 4th Edition:
    The Original Guide to American Cocktails and Drinks (2001)
Caribe Rum: The Original Guide to Caribbean Rum and Drinks (2001)
Successful Beverage Management: Proven Strategies for the On-Premise Operator (2000)
Increasing Bar Sales: Creative Twists to Bigger Profits (1997)
Reducing Bar Costs: A Survival Plan for the 90's (1993)
501 Questions Every Bartender Should Know How to Answer (1993)
The Professional Guide to Bartending — 2nd Edition (1991)
The Intervention Handbook: The Legal Aspects of Serving Alcohol — 2nd Edition (1990)

Publisher & Managing Editor:	Robert Plotkin
Editor & Production Manager:	Carol Plotkin
Cover Design:	Carol Plotkin, Miguel Castillo
Book Design:	Miguel Castillo

Published by: **BarMedia**

P.O. Box 14486
Tucson, AZ 85732
520.747.8131
www.BarMedia.com

ISBN: 0-945562-24-1

Printed in the U.S.A.

Dedication
To Carol Ann Plotkin,
the woman who stole my heart and won't give it back.
RP

Preventing Internal Theft

A Bar Owner's Guide

Table of Contents

Continued on next page

INTRODUCTION

Admittedly, the subject matter of this book is rather sobering. The reality is that many bartenders steal, not to mention cocktail waitresses, food servers, and managers. Employee theft, if left unchecked, can decimate a business's bottom line. The information in this book is intended to help a bar owner or beverage manager detect and limit the losses attributable to employee theft.

What this book is not meant to be is a sweeping professional indictment. Certainly not all bartenders steal. You will not find a single reference in this book suggesting that even the majority of bartenders, or other front-of-house employees, steal from their employers or rip-off the operations' clientele. In fact, adopting a suspicious, malevolent attitude toward your employees can create or exacerbate the very problem you're looking to alleviate. It would be a profound mistake if you were to begin suspecting all of your employees of theft.

Internal theft is, however, a reality. It is an unseen phenomenon and a subject that is hardly ever discussed openly, no less identified as an ongoing operational problem. Yet, the fact remains that food and beverage operations lose an extraordinary amount of income and inventory to internal theft. Learning how to reduce the incidence of theft eventually becomes a prime business consideration for management in this industry.

Bars and restaurants are extremely vulnerable to theft by its employees. Bartenders usually draw the most suspicion, with just cause. They are nearly autonomous employees often working without direct supervision. Bartenders steal from their employers and the establishments' clientele because it's easily accomplished, hard to detect, and nearly impossible to prevent on an ongoing basis. Bartenders can significantly augment their take home earnings by diverting just a small percentage of the operations cash proceeds from the register to the tip jar.

The opportunities are rife for internal theft behind a bar. Recent technological advances, such as video surveillance cameras, electronic liquor dispensers, point-of-sale (P.O.S.) systems, and computerized inventory systems, besides being very capital-intensive investments, will only realistically dissuade the casual thief. A bartender intent on stealing from a bar can successfully circumvent these electronic controls.

The only real challenge most bartenders encounter is exercising restraint in limiting the amount they steal from the operation on a regular basis. The temptations posed by constantly handling large sums of cash and dealing with a liquid inventory can often prove overwhelming. At some point, most people working behind a bar contemplate stealing cash, giving out free drinks, or any one of a multitude of transgressions.

Compounding the problem, few bar owners or beverage managers want to admit to the possibility that their employees might be stealing from them. It's only human nature to want to think the best of people who have been placed in positions of trust. Yet, it is incumbent upon management to make a concerted effort to defend against and limit the losses attributable to internal theft. A thieving bartender can literally steal a business into financial submission by siphoning off the operation's life-sustaining cash flow, depleting the bar's liquor inventory, and defrauding the establishment's clientele. Effectively limiting internal theft is often a matter of economic survival.

Of the three-step program covered in this text to deal with the problem, the first line of defense is to attempt to understand what motivates employees to knowingly defy the risks and steal from a business. By scrutinizing the underlying psychological processes involved, it may be possible to effectively stop some theft before it ever occurs.

The all-important second line of defense involves closely examining the numerous methods bartenders and servers employ to steal from a business. Leaning how to identify likely "targets of opportunity," as well as spotting how employees manipulate an operation for their benefit is important to the process of combating theft. There are over twenty major types of illicit and fraudulent practices bartenders and servers use against a business. Possessing the ability to spot specific improprieties behind the bar is a crucial aspect of the overall defensive strategy.

The third and final line of defense is to establish, implement, and enforce preventative measures that make internal theft more involved to attempt and more difficult to accomplish without detection. While total prevention is realistically improbable, management can still take constructive steps to ensure that employee theft is kept to an absolute minimum.

Inevitably the objection is raised that spending time and effort to prevent bartenders from stealing is a bad investment. Actually preventing employee theft altogether is unlikely, so why bother? "How much money are we really talking about here?" they'll say. Or, "My managers and I have better ways to spend our time than to try and catch a bartender who's pocketing a few bucks here or there. It's almost expected."

Tolerating theft is bad business. To begin with, a bartender can embezzle hundreds of dollars per week. If several bartenders work in concert, the damages can run in the thousands of dollars. Those losses may spell the difference between financial success and failure.

Secondly, tolerating employee theft rapidly destroys morale and diminishes respect for management. Those employees who are doing their jobs honestly will resent their co-workers who do steal. It's human nature. They will also lose respect for their managers who are too blind to notice what's going on behind the bar, or simply don't care. Either way, the honest employees feel like they're in the minority, the moral few who perform their duties with integrity and eschew the attraction of easy money.

Adopting a posture of zero-tolerance is essential to attaining a successful, profitable beverage operation. It requires a dedicated effort, one in which all of the employees and managers share a common vision and work diligently toward common goals. Bartenders who steal from the business or its guests are a negative force. They work according to hidden agendas that are diametrically opposed to those of the business and its staff.

Among your house rules must be, "Don't give into temptation, always run an honest till."

Chapter 1

EXPLORING THE CAUSES OF THEFT

There is an adage in this business that you can tell how much a bartender is going to steal from you each month by finding out the amount of the person's car payment. It's part of the old school of thought, the same one that contends all bartenders are thieves. The problem with that point of view, however, is that it doesn't conform with reality.

With few exceptions, bartenders do not begin working at a new place of employment with the preconceived notion of stealing from the establishment. It is much more likely that employees begin their working relationship with a genuine desire to perform up to professional standards and expectations. Something, therefore, must cause a person to radically change his or her feelings and attitude towards the thought of stealing from his or her employer.

People who are competent and intelligent enough to be hired as a bartender must realize that they would be immediately terminated if caught stealing. Along with the prospect of being fired, employees have to believe that they will lose their job reference, and possibly face further legal consequence, not to mention arrest.

Before someone starts stealing from his or her employer, two important things need to take happen. First, the person will most likely have to justify the act as something other than outright theft. Few people are capable of comfortably betraying their employer's trust in such a profound way. The rationalization process affords them the luxury of redefining theft into terms they are more comfortable with.

Secondly, the employee must consider the act of stealing worth the inherent risk involved. In their minds, bartenders and servers must assess the probability of getting caught to be acceptable when compared to the potential financial gains.

THE PROCESS OF RATIONALIZING THEFT

The justifications used by employees, of course, will vary with the individual, but there seem to be three, reoccurring types of rationalization bartenders and servers rely upon to justify stealing from their employer.

- **Financial Need** — One of the more difficult aspects of being a bartender or server is that a disproportionate amount of the take-home pay is in the way of cash tips. Learning how to budget a cash income on a monthly basis is significantly more challenging than living within one's budget when the income is received in a weekly paycheck. Many employees never learn how to budget their cash earnings. It is therefore not unlikely that they will regularly find themselves financially pressed to meet their monthly obligations, such as rent or car payments. For many, personal finances become so pressing and immediate that stealing money becomes the least complicated remedy to deal with the situation. These employees steal simply because it's an expedient source of supplemental income. Instead of finding a legitimate solution to their problem, they rationalize that stealing the money they need is more a matter of economic survival than a question of propriety or ethical behavior.

- **Larceny and Greed** — Many bartenders steal simply because they perceive it as a daring and illicit act. They receive a sense of gratification when defying the odds, employing guile and cunning, and in the end, prevailing. These employees justify theft as an exciting diversion from the mundane and humdrum. For others, it's not the thrill or excitement that is so alluring about internal theft, it's nothing more complicated than greed. They just want the money, pure and simple.

- **Resentment** — Occasionally, employees might interpret a managerial directive or decision as being unfair or unjust. Perhaps they feel as if they are being treated wrongfully, or that their ability to make a decent livelihood is being infringed upon. Regardless of the reason, hidden resentment is subtle in its capacity to completely undermine an employee's professional attitude, as well as erasing any notion of right or wrong. Resentment is a silent, smoldering emotion. It often surfaces in dark, unseen ways. When an employee bears ill will towards an establishment or its management, theft eventually becomes a constant companion. It offers the person a path of least resistance to rectify the situation. What better way to exact revenge and balance the scales than to deliberately siphon-off the beverage operation's cash flow? Resentment can make most people indignant to feeling any qualms of guilt.

From a managerial perspective, harbored resentment is the most serious and has the potential of being the most financially damaging of the three justifications listed above. Once the pressing nature of an employee's financial situation abates, so may the incidence of internal theft. Likewise, as the lure and excitement of larceny subside, theft may no longer be deemed sufficiently worth the risk.

But time does not necessarily diminish the bitterness of resentment. It can linger undetected for a very long time. In some cases, time only serves to make an individual more spiteful. The longer an employee's attitude problem goes undiagnosed, the more severe the possible financial ramifications will be and the better the chance that the employee's resentment will infect others.

Any long-term strategy aimed at limiting internal theft behind a bar must be coupled with an understanding of the aforementioned psychological motivations. After all, a person doesn't suddenly wake up one morning and decide to start stealing from his or her employer. On the contrary, employees need impetus to overcome their reluctance to place their employment in jeopardy. This motivation is extremely important for management to identify.

Relying solely on specific policies and procedures to combat internal theft behind the bar could prove to be far too short-sighted to achieve positive, tangible results. The effectiveness of those specific measures, however, can be significantly enhanced when accompanied by a corresponding effort to eliminate the underlying motivations behind employee theft. Consequently, it is in management's best interest to do everything within reason to ensure that resentment has no cause to exist on a bartending staff. Mismanaging employees is one sure method of rapidly precipitating internal theft, and therefore, is something which must be diligently avoided.

In addition, bartending applicants must be screened carefully before hiring, and the staff be trained on a continuous basis to improve their abilities behind the bar. Improved abilities usually translates to the employee's earning capacity increasing, which in turn, dramatically reduces the likelihood of internal theft.

Chapter 2

BARTENDER THEFT

Practically speaking, a beverage operator can't expect to be entirely successful in preventing internal theft. There are far too many ways a bartender can steal from a business and its guests. Yet, being well versed in the various scams and illicit practices bartenders use to steal is invaluable knowledge for a bar manager or owner.

An understanding of how they steal will directly lead to more effective preventative measures being implemented. It is one thing to rip-off a business where upper management is clueless and likely won't uncover the impropriety. It's quite another to steal from a business where the managers and owner know what to look for and are too savvy to be victimized.

This type of strategic information can also be beneficial by making you more capable of spotting specific improprieties when they occur behind the bar. Direct supervision is the most effective means of controlling internal theft. Theft is risky enough without trying to accomplish it while a manager or the owner is hovering about. Being well versed in the various schemes bartenders use to steal, greatly improves the powers of observation.

This section of the book details the various methods bartenders may use to steal. The possible variations on these basic themes are bounded only by the guile and imagination of the perpetrator. In addition to explaining precisely how each technique works, there will also be a notation of whether the method will negatively affect the beverage operation's cost percentages, whether the clientele is victimized in the process, and whether the illicit practice places the business in legal jeopardy.

ILLICIT PRACTICES AND SCHEMES

The justifications used by employees, of course, will vary with the individual, but there seem to be three, reoccurring types of rationalization bartenders and servers rely upon to justify stealing from their employer.

- **Call Substitutions** — This illicit practice involves the bartender selling a customer a mixed drink assumed to be made with a requested premium liquor, when in reality a less expensive call brand liquor is used. The bartender charges the patron the full premium price for the drink, but only rings the sale into the register or P. O. S. at the call price, pocketing the cash difference.

- **Premium Substitutions** — The same results can be achieved by substituting well products for premium brand liquors. Substitutions of this type are easily accomplished primarily because once mixed with other products, the subtle differences of many name brand liquors become sufficiently obscured.

  For example, two people at a cocktail table order a tall Tanqueray and tonic and a double Stoli Screwdriver. The bartender returns to the station and prepares the drinks using well liquor instead of the premium liquors requested. In this case, the bartender is relying on the additional tonic water to mask the taste of the gin and the orange juice to obscure the identity of the vodka. The bartender serves the two drinks and collects cash for the premium drinks. He then enters the transaction as two well drinks and pockets the difference.

  This ploy is rarely attempted when the customer is actually sitting at the bar where the substitution may be observed, or when the liquor is served by itself, such as neat or on-the-rocks, making the substitution easily detected.

- **Other Substitutions** — A variation on this theme is the substitution of a less expensive, similar tasting product for a name-brand liqueur. Here the advantage to the bartender revolves around the frequently large cost difference between the two products. For instance, the difference in cost per ounce between Kahlúa and most low-cost coffee liqueurs can exceed 50%. By using a less expensive coffee liqueur in house drinks or other recipes where the substitution will not be noticed, a bartender can essentially use the cost savings to offset previously stolen inventory.

Substitutions will not negatively affect the bar's cost percentages, but they do victimize the establishment's clientele.

Under-Pouring — The intent behind a bartender under-pouring the alcoholic portion used in a series of drinks is to create a surplus of liquor inventory. This surplus of liquor can then be sold to the clientele, and without recording the sale into the bar's register or P. O. S., the bartender can safely pocket the cash proceeds from the sale(s). For instance, if a bartender poured 1 oz. of liquor into a series of four drinks instead of the specified 1 1/4 oz., a surplus of 1 oz. would result. That ounce of liquor could then be sold, and as long as the sale remains unrecorded, the bartender would be free to keep the cash proceeds.

This type of under-pouring does not negatively impact pour cost. In the illustration above, the bartender depleted 5 oz. of liquor and rang-in four sales. Unfortunately, however, five guests' drinks contained less than the prescribed amount of liquor.

• **Ghosting** — Another technique of creating a surplus liquor inventory is called "ghosting". This method entails the bartender deliberately preparing a frozen concoction with less than the required portion of liquor. In fact, sometimes no liquor is used at all. It is extremely difficult for most people to discern how much alcohol is present in frozen drinks because of the large proportion of ice used. Many blended drinks are also made with pureed fruit which will mask the liquor deficiency even more.

• **Floating** — Floating is another method of under-pouring. It entails preparing a basic highball drink by pouring the mixer in first and then floating a 1/2 or 3/4 oz. of liquor on top. The customer's first taste of the drink will seem alcoholically potent and the underage will go unnoticed.

- **Jigger Switch** — Another illicit practice is to secretly switch the size of the bar's measuring device. Most establishments use a standard stainless steel or glass measuring device. These measures are produced in many different sizes and one metal jigger is virtually indistinguishable from the next. If the bartender were to switch a 3/4 oz. measure for the operation's 1 oz. shot, a surplus of 1 oz. would be created with every fourth drink prepared. To facilitate an under-pouring scheme, bartenders have been known to put clear epoxy inside stainless steel jiggers, thereby effectively reducing the measure's capacity. At the end of the night, the regular measure is replaced and the larceny goes undetected.

- **Diluting** — A bartender can instantly create a surplus of inventory by adding tap water to the bar's distilled spirits. If 3 or 4 oz. of water are added to several of the beverage operation's liquor inventory, a bartender can safely sell the same volume of the bar's liquor and pocket the proceeds. Water is extremely difficult to detect in liquor when added in moderation, as it will not affect the taste, aroma, color, or apparent alcoholic potency.

  A devious bartender can actually use this scheme to make the bar's pour cost percentages drop. For example, the bartender can sell a dozen unrecorded drinks made with well liquor. At close, when deemed safe to do so, he can fill a 12 oz. tumbler glass with water and add it to different bottles of premium liquor. By stealing the well liquor and tapping-up the premium liquor, pour cost would be positively affected, thereby causing it to drop.

- **Reportioning** — Finally, a surplus of alcohol can result from the re proportioning of tropical or house specialty drinks. For instance, how many customers would be able to perceive that less rum was used in the preparation of a Zombie or Mai Tai? Bartenders can manipulate the establishment's house specialty drinks in the same manner. Most people do not have a preconceived notion of how house drinks should taste, so if less than the reciped amount of liquor is used, the omission will more than likely go unnoticed.

Under-pouring will not negatively affect the beverage operation's cost percentages which is one reason why it is so prevalent. This practice does victimize the establishment's clientele.

The "Looking the Other Way" Fee — This scheme can potentially have disastrous ramifications for a food and beverage operation. It entails the bartender accepting a cash bribe in return for serving alcohol to someone under legal drinking age, or to an individual who is already intoxicated. Both acts are expressly illegal and can result in the establishment's liquor license being suspended or revoked. In exchange for a few dollars, the bartender places the entire operation in legal jeopardy.

This practice will not affect the operation's cost percentages, but will have long-term legal ramifications.

Drinking On-Duty — When bartenders help themselves to the beverage operation's liquor inventory and drink behind the bar, two violations are actually being committed. First, drinking while on-duty is certainly not part of bartenders' job description. As the beverage alcohol inevitably affects the bartender's mental and physical abilities, impairing the person's judgment, reactions, and coordination, the employee is cheating the management out of professional, competent representation behind the bar. The employer has the right to expect the bartending staff to abstain from drinking alcohol while on-duty. Secondly, the bartender is legitimately stealing the liquor inventory he or she consumes.

- **Abuse of Trust** — Another method bartenders use to abuse their position of trust is to serve alcoholic beverages to other employees while they are on-duty. This is done either to improve their social standing or to receive a better tip-out at the end of the shift. A more mercenary variation involves the bartender actually selling alcoholically-laced beverages at greatly reduced prices to fellow employees during the course of an evening. Bartenders have even been known to negotiate with the kitchen staff, trading liquor for food.

Many operations allow their employees to drink at the bar after they have clocked out and ended their shift. While this may afford the employees with an opportunity to socialize with other employees, it also creates an ideal scenario for theft. For example, the bartender can give fellow employees free drinks, discounted drinks, or drinks with excessively large portions of alcohol. The bartender may also sell the employees premium drinks at well prices.

Bartenders drinking alcohol while on-duty will certainly negatively affect the beverage operation's cost percentages. In states in which it is illegal for bartenders to drink alcohol while on-duty, the practice may place the establishment in legal jeopardy.

Inventory Abuse — Bartenders who tamper with the inventory can create a number of lucrative opportunities to increase their personal net worth. One method of stealing entails a bartender claiming that a full liter of liquor was accidentally broken. In reality, the bartender will take an empty bottle, break it, and then present that to the manager. Since some breakage behind a commercial bar is unavoidable, there is not much that management can do other than issue a replacement bottle of liquor and urge the bartender to be more careful with the inventory in the future. That replacement bottle represents a liquor inventory surplus behind the bar of 33.8 oz. The bartender can take advantage of that surplus by selling the alcohol and pocketing the cash proceeds.

Establishments that use bartenders to expedite the process of taking physical inventory of the bar are leaving themselves open for the employees to record faulty data. If the bartender conducting the physical inventory consistently overstates the amount of liquor on-hand at the end of the month, it will have the effect of understating the month's liquor usage. For example, if a bottle of Absolut was one-quarter full, but the bartender recorded that it was three-quarters full, he would have inflated the ending inventory by half a liter, or just over 16 oz.

The bartender could have two motives for this. If he was engaged in stealing unrecorded drinks, overstating the inventory by a half-liter would off-set the theft of sixteen, 1 oz. drinks. The other reason might be to inflate the inventory readings so that when management takes that information to calculate the bar's cost percentages, the pour cost derived will be significantly lower than it legitimately should have been. This will make the bar seem more efficient and profitable than it actually is, creating a favorable impression of the bartending staff and glossing over previous improprieties.

- **Smuggling** — Another scheme used by bartenders to defraud an establishment is to smuggle full bottles of liquor into the bar. The smuggled products are frequently the same name-brand liquors used in the beverage operation's well. As before, this practice will automatically create a surplus liquor inventory which the bartender can then sell and keep the unrecorded proceeds.

  For example, a bartender smuggles a pint flask—16 oz.—of well vodka behind the bar. He proceeds to sell sixteen, 1 oz. drinks for $3 each and pockets the proceeds. Then sometime prior to leaving he secretly pours the flask of vodka into a bottle of well vodka, replacing the stolen inventory and leaving pour cost unaffected. If he paid six dollars for the pint of vodka, he would turn a quick profit of $42.

  Many larger hotels and resorts use bottle tagging as a method of liquor inventory control. These tags are affixed to the liquor bottles so that management can readily identify each specific bottle. This practice is intended to stop bartenders from secretly bringing in bottles of liquor into the operation. This system can break down if the tags are not diligently monitored and checked on a regular basis. Bartenders can abuse the system by removing the tags from legitimately issued bottles and reapplying them onto products smuggled into the operation for their own personal gain.

Abusing the inventory will not negatively impact the operation's cost percentages. Since it is nearly universally true that it is illegal for a beverage operation to sell liquor originally purchased from a non-approved source this scheme involving smuggled inventory can place the business's liquor license in legal jeopardy.

Banquet and Catering Abuse — Many food and beverage operations eventually expand into on-site and off-site catering. As most of these catered events require a full bar set-up, it makes sense to use the existing bartending staff to man the bars at these functions. Catered functions, however, typically operate with few inventory and cash controls, and the bartenders operate with little or no direct supervision. Precautions must be taken to prevent the bartender(s) from smuggling liquor inventory from the banquet into the establishment's main bar. This can easily be accomplished by either stealing full bottles or drawing off the liquor into separate containers. Once a bartender has brought liquor behind the bar, there is little chance of detecting the illicit transfer of inventory. The bartenders are then free to sell the liquor and pocket the unrecorded proceeds, or use the inventory to offset previous theft.

A large percentage of catered functions are set up as cash bars, where the patrons pay for their drinks. This requires the bartender to handle cash, and more often than not, he or she is not required to use a cash register. As a result, the bartender is in a position to siphon-off cash without being burdened by the problem of how to work around the register.

Banquet and catering abuses will not negatively affect the beverage operation's cost percentages. They will, however, decimate the catered function's profit margins.

Misuse of Promotional Material — In an effort to stimulate business, many establishments use promotional devices, such as chits or coupons, that customers can redeem for free drinks. Bartenders often have easy access to these promotional chits, which in the hands of a thief, become a convenient means of covering up internal theft. Bartenders can take advantage of this type of promotional device by selling a drink, pocketing the cash proceeds, and depositing a free drink coupon into the cash register or P.O.S. drawer.

This type of fraud will not negatively impact the bar's cost percentages.

Overcharging Guests — The establishment's clientele can also be the unwitting victims of theft. One time-tested means of defrauding a customer involves a bartender overcharging a patron for a drink, ringing in the legitimate price, and pocketing the cash difference.

Buck Boosting — Another method of ripping off the clientele is called "buck boosting." Frequently, when a patron is ready to leave, the person will tell the bartender that he or she is ready to clear the bar tab. Without actually showing the customer the bar check, the bartender will tell the guest how much is due. The illicit twist is that the bartender will quote a dollar amount higher than what was rung-up into the cash register or P. O. S. Typically the customer will accept the quoted amount as legitimate and pay the tab. The bartender can then deposit the appropriate amount of money into the register or P. O. S., and pocket the cash difference. If the patron asks to see the drink check, and notices the discrepancy, the bartender can claim that the quoted amount was a mistake and the incident is all but forgotten.

Bogus Items — Bartenders can also steal from the clientele by adding bogus purchases to a patron's drink tab. People frequently don't scrutinize their tabs before paying, merely accepting the ticket total as accurate. In this case, since the fraudulent charges were recorded into the cash register, the total amount collected from the customer will need to be deposited. This can be used to the bartender's advantage by offsetting previous theft. In addition, since the bartender is usually tipped-out based on the dollar amount of the drink tab, inflating the total will have a positive affect on the gratuity received.

A variation on the theme involves the bartender pocketing cash for unrecorded drinks, and charging those drinks off to another customer's tab, again assuming that the patron won't carefully check the bill. Once the customer pays his or her tab, the theft is covered and pour cost is left unaffected.

> *Overcharging will not negatively impact the operation's cost percentages, but it obviously will adversely affect the establishment's clientele.*

Cash Register and P.O.S. Abuse — A creative technique to steal money out of the register is to clear the machine by taking a "Z" reading an hour or so before last call. By clearing the register with an hour of sales remaining, everything sold during that period of time can be rung up directly into the machine and safely pocketed after everyone has left for the night. While electronic cash registers and P.O.S. imprint the time the "Z" reading was taken onto the transactional tape, few managers or owners make note of it.

The bartender has only to clear the register again and dispose of the second "Z" reading tape. The transactional tape from the first "Z" reading is submitted along with the night's deposits, less of course, the money generated during the last hour of sales, leaving behind no evidence of theft.

• **False Overrings** — Another method of using the operation's cash register to defraud the business is a technique involving "make-up rings." An example of a "make-up ring" would be a bartender, intending to ring up a $3.50 sale into the register, mistakenly enters $3.00. To correct the error, the employee rings up another fifty cents into the machine so that the deposit matches the register's sales figures.

A bartender can use "make-up rings" by purposely making an error entering a transaction. For instance, a bartender could sell an $8.50 drink and only ring $.50 into the cash register, pocketing the unrecorded $8.00. If the bartender is questioned about the transaction at some later time, he or she can claim that the $.50 entry was a "make-up ring" for a previous transaction.

These illicit practices involving the cash register negatively affect the beverage operation's cost percentages.

Soft Drink Abuse — Fruit juices and fountain drinks are typically not inventoried items. These products, therefore, are behind the bar without any standard means of control. This gives the bartender access to abuse these products. A bartender can sell several soft drinks and either keep the unrecorded cash proceeds, or ring the transaction into the register as a liquor sale. This will have the effect of padding the liquor sales for the night, offsetting previous theft.

This method of stealing will negatively impact the beverage operation's cost percentages.

Double Use of Drink Tickets — This technique takes advantage of the fact that one drink ticket is virtually indistinguishable from another, and thus it is nearly impossible to detect if a particular ticket has been fraudulently reused. This operational weakness can be exploited by a bartender who secretly keeps a stash of tickets which have been previously rung up into the cash register. A bartender using this method of theft will have imprinted tickets covering several different drink price combinations. The bartender has only to present one of the drink tickets to a patron that corresponds exactly to the customer's own drink order, both in dollar amount and number of drinks served.

This is easier to accomplish than it may sound. Often two people, for example, will order two rounds of well drinks. A bar ticket is then tabulated to reflect four well drinks sold at the well liquor price. That particular bar ticket could be reused at a later time to rip-off the proceeds of an identical drink order. The customer would notice nothing suspicious, pay the amount on the drink check, and leave. The bartender is then free to keep the unrecorded sale and reuse the ticket again if the opportunity arises.

- **Changing Tickets** — Handwritten drink tickets can be altered after the customer has paid a tab. A bartender could change the ticket to reflect a lower check amount than what was collected, the second dollar amount is rung into the register, and the difference in cash goes to the employee. A slight variation on this theme involves a bartender making a premeditated mathematics error in calculating the drink check total. If the customer notices the mistake, it can easily be chalked up as an honest miscalculation. If the error goes unnoticed, the bartender will simply correct the mistake, deposit the appropriate amount of money into the cash register, and keep the difference.

- **Voiding Tickets** — Another method of abusing drink tickets for personal gain entails the bartender getting the manager-on-duty to void a previously rung-in drink ticket, claiming the transaction had been entered into the cash register incorrectly. For instance, a bartender shows the manager two sequentially numbered drink tickets. The first ticket, the lower numbered check, is for two premium mixed drinks totaling $9, which is actually the amount of money the bartender collected from the patron. The second ticket is imprinted with a sale of two well drinks for a total of $6. The bartender claims that the second ticket reflects the actual sale and that the first check needs to be voided as an error. Since it appears the bartender mistakenly rang-in two premium drinks instead of two well drinks, the manager will likely void the first ticket and the employee is free to keep the $3 difference.

All of the aforementioned practices will negatively impact the beverage operation's cost percentages.

Spillage and "Comp." Drink Abuse — Spillage is an unavoidable, uncontrollable cost of doing business. Customers, food servers, cocktail servers, and bartenders can all legitimately cause liquor to be spilled or wasted. The spillage sheet is an operational form used to record any liquor depleted from inventory without a corresponding cash sale. The spillage sheet, over the course of the inventory period, will quantify the cost of liquor wasted.

A bartender can take advantage of the spillage sheet by using the form to cover-up theft by recording the stolen liquor as accidentally spilled. For example, the bartender can sell an unrecorded drink, pocket the cash proceeds, and log the drink as spilled with the knowledge that the theft will not adversely impact the bar's pour cost.

The "comp" drink sheet is an operational form used to track the cost of the complimentary drinks given away to the clientele over a specified inventory period. The system, however, can be used to off-set the theft of unrecorded drinks. For example, a bartender approaches the manager-on-duty seeking approval to "comp." two guests a round of drinks. The manager agrees and signs the "comp." drink sheet. When the couple orders another round, the bartender serves the drinks and pockets the cash proceeds, safe in the knowledge that the drinks have already been accounted for and that pour cost will not be affected.

Because the information posted on these two operational forms are factored into the bar's cost percentages, these scams will not negatively affect the operation's pour cost.

Draft Beer Abuse — Implementing effective controls on your draft beer is essential. On a national average, retailers lose approximately 20% of the draft beer they purchase due to waste, spillage and employee theft.

There are several factors that make draft beer an attractive window of opportunity for thieves. Many bartenders fully understand that standard cost analysis and sales projections cannot be accurately derived for draft beer. As a result, bartenders can give away draft beer or sell it to customers and pocket the proceeds with little chance of suspicions being raised. Most establishments regularly waste so much draft beer that theft is virtually impossible to isolate.

Likewise, a bartender could serve several draft beers, deposit the proceeds, and ring-up the transaction into liquor sales, compensating for previous theft.

These fraudulent practices will negatively affect the beverage operation's beer cost percentage, as well as possibly distorting the liquor pour cost.

Over-Pouring — Typically, bartenders over-pour a standard portion of liquor in a customer's drink to attempt to receive a better tip. Many bartenders operate under the faulty assumption that if they serve guests overly-potent drinks their chances of receiving better tips will drastically improve. More often than not, it doesn't work that way.

The fact that over-pouring will have a marked impact on the patron's sobriety, or that over-pouring the establishment's standard liquor portion is outright theft is little deterrent when compared with the lure of a better tip.

One of the difficult aspects of over-pouring is that most bartenders do not consider it outright theft. It is, however, for two important reasons. Over-pouring not only robs you of inventory, it bleeds away your profit margin. For example, instead of pouring the specified portion of 1 1/4 oz., a bartender serves a drinks with 1 3/4 oz. and charges the guest the normal sales price of $5.00. If the liquor costs 86 cents an ounce, the portion cost for the drink rose from $1.08 ($.86 X 1.25) to $1.51 ($.86 X 1.75), an increase in cost of $.43, and a drop in the profit margin of nearly 40%.

The second cost associated with over-pouring is the opportunity cost. Over-pouring alcohol will inevitably accelerate a patron's level of inebriation and a bring about a hasty departure. In the illustration above, after the third, overly potent drink, the patron will have consumed more alcohol than contained in three, regularly prepared drinks, a loss of one retail sale, or $5.00.

Over-pouring will have a definite negative affect on the beverage operation's cost percentage as well as promoting over consumption of alcohol.

Short Changing — One of the more obvious scams bartenders use to defraud an establishment is to short-change its clientele. This practice is predicated on the observation that customers typically will not take the time to verify their change. While some guests would likely notice if they were short a five- or ten-dollar bill, others, especially those feeling the effects of alcohol, likely will not. If the person did happen to catch the shortage, the bartender would shake his head in dismay, and claim that it was an inadvertent error.

The same result can be achieved by the bartender deftly snaring an unsuspecting customer's change off the bar top.

While short-changing will have no affect on the bar's cost percentages, it does defraud the establishment's clientele.

Unrecorded Sales — This is the grand daddy of them all. Theft through unrecorded sales is the most prevalent method of internal theft behind a bar. Why? To begin with, it is the most obvious form of theft, totally lacking in ingenuity or creativity. It is the first scam that occurs to bartenders. It is also the easiest type of theft. It's quick, uncomplicated and there's little deception involved.

The most basic form of theft involving unrecorded sales is a bartender giving away free drinks. It does, of course, rob you of your liquor inventory. Compounding the loss, giving away a free drink deprives the operation of the revenue stemming from the sale of that particular drink to the customer.

- **Give It Away** — Most bartenders consider giving away a free drink a cost of doing business, a type of promotional expense. They see it as giving away a few quarters worth of product in exchange for generating good will for the bar, as well as a better tip for themselves. Unfortunately, few bartenders have an accurate understanding of the actual cost of the products you carry in your inventory. They also don't consider the opportunity cost of their actions. For example, a bartender gives away a drink made with a jigger of liquor that costs 86 cents per ounce and normally retails for $5.00. The actual cost associated with giving away that drink is $1.29 ($.86 X 1.5 oz.) in liquor, plus the lost retail sale of $5.00, equaling $6.29.

Unrecorded sales often occur when a patron is running a drink tab. A bartender can ingratiate himself with a customer by purposely not ringing up each drink served. Theoretically, these omissions would occur for the purpose of securing a better gratuity from the customer benefiting from the unrecorded sales.

- **Sell It to the Bartender** — The next logical step up from giving away unrecorded drinks is selling them. In this case, a bartender serves a mixed drink, collects the cash proceeds of the sale, but instead of recording the transaction and depositing the funds, the bartender keeps the money.

- **The "No Sale" Key** — It is imperative for thieving bartenders, while on-duty, to conform to operating procedures and not raise suspicions. This begs the questions then, what do they do with all of the stolen cash? Stuffing their pockets full of currency would be ridiculous. Likewise, cramming money into their tip jar would be far too obvious. Therefore, the only safe repository for the ill-gotten gains is the one spot where the money was intended to be deposited in the first place, the cash drawer of the register or P.O.S. To illustrate, a bartender serves two drinks and collects the cash proceeds. The anticipated response is for the bartender to turn and address the cash register or P.O.S., anything else would appear suspicious. Since the bartender cannot afford to enter transactional data into one of the register's sales keys, the "No Sale" key is the most commonly used method to get the cash register's drawer open without being self-defeating. Few people actually pay close attention to the cash register's L.C.D. display. If they did, they may very well be surprised to learn how frequently a Bloody Mary or Singapore Sling is rung-up as a "No Sale."

- **"Juggling" Drink Orders** — This technique, referred to as "juggling," entails a bartender collecting money for drinks from two or more customers at once. The collected cash from all of the transactions are deposited into the register, but only one of the sales is rung-up into the machine. The money received for the unrecorded sales can be retrieved by the bartender from the cash register's drawer at a safe, opportune time and pocketed.

  Unrecorded sales will negatively affect the beverage operation's cost percentages.

Undercharging Guests — What are the odds that the bartender's friends seated at the bar are paying full-price for their drinks? Undercharging friends and regular customers is a scam often used by bartenders to either reward patronage, or to improve their social standing with friends.

  Undercharging for drinks will have a negative impact on the beverage operation's cost percentages.

Fake Walk-Outs — Customers skipping out on their drink or food tabs is a regrettable fact of life. Typically the establishment absorbs the loss and the server is reminded to be more attentive to the guests. A bartender can take advantage of the situation by collecting cash for a party's drink tab, and after the group has left, claim to the manager that they left without clearing their tab. There's nothing that the manager can do about rectifying the situation at that point, and the bartender is free to pocket the cash.

  Fake walk-outs will negatively affect the beverage operation's cost percentages.

Bank Fraud — Managers are not infallible, and they have been known to make mistakes assembling the bar's opening banks. It is standard procedure that bartenders be required to verify the amount of their opening banks. A bartender, however, could pocket ten or twenty dollars and claim that the bank was short by that amount. There would be little that the management could do but replace the shortage.

This type of bank fraud will not have an impact on the beverage operation's cost percentages.

Time Clock Abuse — Theft need not always involve the beverage operation's inventory or cash. Bartenders can also steal from the business using a technique called "riding the clock". They can accrue additional payroll hours by improperly staying on-duty longer than is actually required, or by taking more time than necessary to break down the bar at closing.

Another method used by employees to conspire together to cheat the operation involves one employee surreptitiously clocking-in for another employee who has not yet actually reported for work. Each of these practices rob the establishment of funds by inflating payroll expenditures.

Neither technique detailed will have any affect on the beverage operation's cost percentages, but will adversely affect service payroll.

SUMMARY

Everett Dirkson, the famed United States Senator, perhaps said it best. "A billion here and a billion there, and pretty soon you're talking about some real money!"

It could be said that the scams and illicit practices detailed in this chapter are nothing but "penny ante" schemes that really don't amount to much. After all, what's a few dollars here or there? Isn't "shrinkage" an anticipated cost of doing business?

"Shrinkage" should never be tolerated, and it certainly isn't an acceptable business expense. As for its potential negative effect, consider the following illustration, a bartender employed at a high volume establishment who is scheduled to work five, seven-hour shifts per week. Using many of the techniques described in this chapter, he looks to rip-off the house about twenty dollars per hour, or $140 per shift. His larceny would amount to roughly $700 per week, or $2,800 per month. Far fetched? Not at all.

Are there scams and illicit practices that bartenders can use to steal other than those described in this chapter? Unless bartenders are given access to the business check book, a set of master keys and the combination to the safe, the most probable answer is no. There are a finite number of ways that bartenders can employ to rip-off the house with a reasonable assurance that their transgressions will go undetected.

Essentially, there are approximately two dozen areas of vulnerability that can be exploited behind the bar. Bartenders can give away free drinks, over-charge or under-charge the clientele, pocket the sales proceeds of unrecorded drinks, substitute well liquor for call brands, under-pour or over-pour liquor portions, reuse drink tickets, or off-set their crimes by altering inventory systems or enter false sales data into the cash register or P.O.S. They can cover theft by inflating the inventory through smuggling-in product or watering the liquor, voiding transactions, or simply clearing out the register early. They can drink on-duty, or slip drinks to co-workers and friends. Everything else is a creative variation on the theme.

Ironically, one of the main reasons the schemes outlined in this chapter are as effective as they are is that the majority of bartenders conduct themselves in a professional and ethical manner. If the percentage of bartenders who were actively engaged in stealing were to dramatically increase, bar owners and beverage managers would naturally become more suspicious and the establishments' clientele would grow increasingly more wary.

Chapter 3

PREVENTATIVE MEASURES

Effectively limiting internal theft behind the majority of bars is no easy task, and eliminating it altogether is unrealistic. Regardless of the difficulty factor involved, you must formulate and implement an operational strategy for containing the problem.

There is an adage in this business that states, "A quarter of your employees will steal from you, while a quarter will conduct themselves honesty. The other half will only be as honest as they need to be." Like all sweeping generalities, this adage should not be taken literally. Its underlying message, however, contains sound advice that should be heeded. The message is that you need to anticipate that roughly three out of four employees steal to some degree. Unfortunately, this adage seems most applicable to the bar.

This chapter deals exclusively with the complex issue of reducing bartender theft. There are several approaches that need to be taken to affect any significant impact on the problem. The first involves putting specific analytical devices in place that will provide you with a detailed financial picture of what's going on behind your bar. These devices are indispensable tools and will provide you with numerous operational benefits.

The strategy also involves implementing an effective inventory control system. The intent of the system is to allow you to track inventory from the point of purchase through the audit cycle until the items are depleted. The system advanced in this chapter will let you know conclusively what you have in inventory, what you paid for it, where it is, and at what rate it's used. A complete and detail accounting of the inventory is also critical at detecting and deterring internal theft.

In addition, management must initiate specific measures aimed at alleviating the operation's vulnerability to theft, thereby making it riskier and more difficult for bartenders to steal, while making it easier for you to detect the theft.

The preventative measures mentioned in this chapter are divided into two major sections. The first segment puts forth certain employee policies and procedures formulated to help you better control the operation of the bar. When consistently enforced, these management directives will establish definitive guidelines governing legitimate action and conduct for the bartending staff.

The second section outlines specific preventative measures that you can initiate that address problematic areas of the operation, such as assuring proper portioning, and maintaining effective cash and inventory controls.

SECTION I:
PREVENTION THROUGH BEVERAGE OPERATIONS ANALYSIS AND INVENTORY CONTROL

Perhaps the ultimate means of preventing internal theft would be to set up camp at the bar and observe everything that transpires from the moment the front doors open until well after closing. Direct supervision is about as effective of a theft deterrent as there is. Few bartenders would risk ripping off the house with the owner or bar manager watching.

Uninterrupted supervision of the bar, however, is impractical. Fortunately, there are two methods of analysis that are extremely effective at revealing what is transpiring. They provide a glimpse behind the scenes, a snapshot of every transaction.

Using these two internal analytical devices is sound management. Use every tool at your disposal, and in essence, that's exactly what pour cost and productivity are. Pour cost analyzes the relationship between cost and sales, which not only reveals your operation's profitability, but it often will be an early indication you're getting ripped off.

Tracking employee productivity is equally important. It measures employee performance in terms of sales per hour, and there are two definite benefits to monitoring bartender productivity. If a person's sales per hour are continually higher than the staff average, you'll be in the position to positively acknowledge his or her performance. If, on the other hand, a bartender's productivity steadily falls below the staff average, you may have uncovered the identity of a thief.

POUR COST ANALYSIS:
THE PROFITABILITY BAROMETER

Pour cost—jargon for cost percentage—is a reliable indicator of profit/loss performance and an effective means of detecting internal theft. Pour cost is obtained by dividing the cost of depleted inventory by the gross sales generated over a given period of time.

How often you calculate your bar's pour cost is an important decision. There are establishments that take physical inventories and formulate pour cost daily. Others do so on a weekly, biweekly, or monthly basis. The shorter the amount of time between physical audits, the more insight you'll have into your business. The higher the operation's volume, the more frequently you should take physical audits. If a problem does exist, the sooner it is discovered, the sooner it can be dealt with.

Because liquor, beer and wine sell at radically different cost percentages, each must be calculated separately for the process to have any real significance. Although the following pour cost illustration is for liquor, the same formula applies to any inventory category. In addition, all non-sale depletions of inventory must be factored into the equation. These include any products spilled, wasted, transferred or given out in complimentary drinks.

To illustrate the process, suppose your operation's beginning monthly liquor inventory is determined to be $8,900. Over the course of the month you purchased an additional $3,350 in liquor. The Adjusted Beginning Inventory is arrived at by adding the two figures together ($12,250) and represents the total cost of the liquor inventory for the entire month.

At the end of the month you conduct another physical audit and establish that the value of the ending liquor inventory is $7,050. Having kept track of all non-sale depletions, you add the cost of the month's spillage ($19), transfers ($33) and complimentary drinks ($68) to the ending inventory thereby negating these factors as variables. The resulting figure of $7,170 is the Adjusted Ending Liquor Inventory, the cumulative cost of the liquor on-premise at the end of the month.

By subtracting the adjusted ending inventory from the adjusted beginning inventory you arrive at the all-important Liquor Cost. It represents the hard cost of all liquor depleted from inventory, in this instance $5,080 ($12,250 - $7,170).

To derive the bar's liquor pour cost, divide the liquor cost ($5,080) by the month's gross liquor sales ($29,300). When multiplied by 100, the resultant (.1734) is converted into 17.34%.

	Beginning Liquor Inventory	**$8,900**	
Add:	Liquor Purchases	$3,350	
	Adjusted Beginning Liquor Inventory		$12,250
	Ending Liquor Inventory	$7,050	
Add:	Cost of waste/spillage	$19	
Add:	Cost of complimentary drinks	$68	
Add:	Cost of transfers	$33	
Subtract:	Adjusted Ending Liquor Inventory		$7,170
	Cost of Depleted Liquor Inventory		$5,080
Divide by:	Gross Liquor Sales		$29,300
Multiply:	Resultant X 100		**17.34%**

A liquor pour cost of 17.34% means that it cost a little more than 17 cents to generate a dollar of liquor sales. It also means that the gross profit margin is 82.66% or just under 83 cents per dollar of sales.

No two beverage operations are the same. Our sample pour cost of 17.34% could be cause for elation or alarm depending on its relationship to the bar's previous performance. Perhaps the single constant in pour cost is that every manager would like to see it move lower; for every percent it decreases, gross profit increases by the same amount.

ANALYZING POUR COST

When pour cost increases, an explanation needs to be found. There are a number of possibilities, the most likely of which include:

- **Physical Inventory Inaccuracies** — Errors in the physical inventory process will provide misleading results. Common mistakes include: inaccurate audit readings; products overlooked and therefore not included in the audit; arithmetic errors; understating liquor inventory wholesale costs; and using inaccurate (understated) liquor sales figures. Any error that causes the ending inventory figure to be understated (making it appear that more inventory was depleted than in actuality) will make pour cost rise.

- **Lagging Sales Prices** — Rising wholesale costs will steadily push pour cost upward. Lowering the costs percentages may require an attendant rise in your drink prices.

- **Poor Ordering and Receiving Procedures** — Inventory purchases should take advantage of wholesale discounts and post-offs whenever possible. Poor ordering and receiving procedures can drive up pour cost; practices such as not carefully inspecting liquor shipments that result in accepting broken product, or product in the wrong quantity, wrong size package or at the wrong price.

- **Promotional Discounting** — Promotions and special drink offers such as "two-for-ones" or serving doubles at regular prices during Happy Hour will basically double the cost percentage for each drink served during the promotion.

- **Shift in Sales Mix Percentage** — A significant shift in your sales mix percentages can cause pour cost to increase. If premium liquors begin selling at a higher rate relative to the well liquor, pour cost will increase. With few exceptions, premium and super premium liquors sell at a much higher cost percentage than do well brands.

- **Drink Portioning** — The staff may be over-portioning drinks, thereby negatively impacting pour cost. Increasing the liquor portion in a drink from 1 oz. to 1 1/4 oz. raises its cost and alcoholic potency 25% per drink.

- **Unrecorded Non-Sale Depletions** — Unrecorded spillage, transfers and complimentary drinks will make the beverage operation appear less efficient and profitable than it actually is. Each results in inventory being depleted without an offsetting sale, which if not accounted for will cause pour cost to increase.

- **Employee Theft** — Internal theft, practices such as selling unrecorded drinks, undercharging for drinks, drinking alcohol behind the bar and giving away free drinks will cause pour cost to increase dramatically.

BAR PRODUCTIVITY:
SPOTTING THE FINGERPRINTS OF THEFT

Tracking pour cost has long been the accepted way of detecting bartender theft. But if you're waiting for pour cost alone to alert you to a potential problem, you may be out of luck. There are more ways to steal from a bar that don't have the slightest affect on pour cost than there are that do. In fact, a clever thief can steal from your bar and actually make your pour cost percentage drop.

When a bartender serves a drink and pockets the cash proceeds, he's basically increasing cost without increasing sales, which is exactly what causes pour cost to rise. While the effect may be imperceptible, the bar's cost percentage will be negatively affected. If, however, the same bartender replaces the stolen liquor with an equal amount of water, pour cost will remain unaffected.

Pour cost is based on liquid volume, meaning that cost of goods sold is predicated on the amount of inventory depleted. If a bartender steals 20 oz. of liquor in a night and later replenishes the inventory with water, the theft will not be detected by analyzing pour cost. In essence, he stole 20 oz. of fluid inventory and then replenished it, a net effect of zero.

Consider what would happen if a bartender were to steal 20 oz. of well liquor over the course of a night, and instead of replenishing the well liquors with water, added the water to a number of premium liquor bottles. Stealing well liquors and off-setting the theft by watering down premium products would actually cause pour cost to drop.

The substitution scam is another example of a type of theft that won't cause pour cost to increase. Again, the scam involves a bartender making the drink with a well liquor instead of a call brand, charging the customer the call price and pocketing the difference. Since the bartender poured well liquor and registered the transaction as a well sale, pour cost will remain unaffected.

Under-pouring schemes are another example. A bartender under-pours a series of four drinks by 1/4 oz., creating a surplus ounce of liquor. The bartender then sells that shot of liquor and pockets the cash. Again, pour cost is unaffected. While measuring your pour cost percentage is a smart thing to do, it's not enough. If the early detection of internal theft is important to you, there's more that you should know.

With nearly all types of theft behind the bar, one thing is certain—the cash proceeds are not ending up in the register. Regardless of the scam, or the subterfuge involved, the money winds up in the bartender's pocket. So to spot the first signs of theft, look at sales.

Bar productivity measures bartender sales per hour, and is computed by dividing the shift's gross sales by the number of hours the bartender worked. There are two aspects to tracking productivity; calculating the staff's average sales per hour figured on a weekly basis, as well as computing the daily sales per hour figures for each shift.

Calculating the staff's productivity involves totaling the bar's gross sales, and dividing it by the total bartenders' payroll hours for the week. It's advisable to calculate the day shift's average sales per hour separately from the night staff's average. Because there is often a considerable difference between the two figures, calculating the day shift's productivity separately from the night makes the process more significant.

For example, if the night bartenders rang-in $6,935 in sales for the week, and clocked-in a combined 83 payroll hours, the staff average for the night crew works out to $83.55 per hour. During the day, the bartending staff rang-in $2,250 is sales and worked 40.5 hours for a staff average of $55.55 per hour.

The second aspect of productivity is tracking sales per hour for each shift during the week. To illustrate, three bartenders work on Thursday night. Jim works 6 hours and rings-in sales of $542.07, or $90.34 per hour. Adam, working 6.5 hours at the same bar on the same night, registers sales of $442.95, which translates to $68.15 per hour.

Keep a journal and track productivity figures for each shift on an on-going basis. After several weeks patterns will emerge. (see inset) It will soon become evident who your sales leaders are, and which employees fall consistently short of the staff average.

Date	Name	Day/Shift	Sales	Hrs	Sales/hr
2/07	Jim	Thurs/PM	$876.35	6.5	$134/hr
	Adam	Thurs/PM	$966.50	6.0	$161/hr
2/14	Jim	Thurs/PM	$799.10	6.5	$123/hr
	Adam	Thurs/PM	$867.38	6.0	$145/hr
2/21	Jim	Thurs/PM	$781.33	6.5	$120/hr
	Adam	Thurs/PM	$903.71	6.0	$151/hr
2/28	Jim	Thurs/PM	$691.85	6.5	$106/hr
	Neil	Thurs/PM	$875.00	6.0	$146/hr
3/07	Jim	Thurs/PM	$745.95	6.5	$115/hr
	Adam	Thurs/PM	$905.00	6.0	$151/hr
3/14	Jim	Thurs/PM	$809.88	6.5	$125/hr
	Adam	Thurs/PM	$898.90	6.0	$150/hr
3/21	Jim	Thurs/PM	$891.95	6.5	$137/hr
	Neil	Thurs/PM	$955.50	6.0	$159/hr

Average Productivity

Jim — 7 shifts at $123/hr

Adam — 5 shifts at $152/hr

Neil — 2 shifts at $153/hr

Weekly Staff Average — 14 PM shifts at $144/hr

ANALYZING PRODUCTIVITY

If a bartender's sales per hour comes in consistently below the staff average, five things are possible. One, he may move too slow and literally can't keep up with demand. Two, he could make lousy drinks, so people don't stick around. Three, his personality and attitude could be so off-putting that customers leave early. Four, his sales ability could be so unrefined that he consistently undersells. Or five, he could be stealing. Each could account for a low sales per hour.

How do you know which it is? Take some time and observe the person. Does he move quickly and with purpose? Or is he more laid back and sluggish? If the person can't keep up behind the bar, then you've identified an area in which he needs to improve.

If that's not a problem, does it appear as if he has the necessary skills for the job? Do his drinks look good, or are they frequently returned? Does the bartender have a good personality for the job? Does it seem as if he has a positive working attitude? Does he exhibit good sales ability? If none of these things seem to be a problem, he may be stealing. Regardless of the scam, theft takes a toll on productivity.

Tracking productivity can prove to be an invaluable management tool. Between pour cost and bar productivity, there isn't a scam or fraud that you can't catch.

INVENTORY CONTROL: CREATING AN INTERNAL AUDIT TRAIL

This is a liquid business—inventory levels behind the bar change with every flick of the bartender's wrist. Controlling costs and limiting exposure to internal theft is solely dependent on knowing precisely what you have, where it is and when you sold it. Achieving that requires accurately monitoring your inventory from the moment it comes through the back door until it's served.

In jargon it's referred to as "cradle to grave" accounting and it involves implementing a series of overlapping internal bookkeeping systems that in concert track every liter through the inventory cycle. While uncompli-cated, the key to the system is ensuring that all of the components are in place and being used properly.

CRADLE TO GRAVE ACCOUNTING

The intent behind implementing a "cradle to grave" accounting system is to track what happens to every product from the moment it enters the back door until its sold, spilled or otherwise depleted from your opera-tion's inventory. Here are the internal systems that allow it to work:

- **Liquor, Beer and Wine Purchase Orders** — Used to record all of the specifics concerning what was ordered; when the delivery arrives, the purchase order provides a means of verifying the legitimacy of the shipment. Each item in the delivery should be physically inspected for damage, to verify the seals are intact and that what was delivered is exactly what was ordered. Only after the delivery has been determined to be complete and correct is the invoice signed, thus formally accepting the merchandise. For security reasons, the delivered products are then immediately stocked into the liquor storeroom or wine room.

  All of the operation's liquor must be stored in a locked and secure area. Every effort must be made to ensure that the inven-tory is as safe as practically possible, including limiting which personnel are granted access to the establishment's liquor room. It is a very sound policy to only permit management access to the liquor room, as there is no viable reason for any employee to be given keys to the liquor room.

- **Perpetual Inventory System** — This internal bookkeeping system is used to track the flow of inventory in and out of the store room. At any point in time, the perpetual inventory system should indicate the exact quantity on-hand for every product stocked. The more inventory on-hand, the more imperative it is that a perpetual system be used. Whenever a product is requisi-tioned from the liquor room, the transaction is recorded on the item's perpetual inventory sheet (or bin card). The requisitioned amount is subtracted from the quantity on-hand as reflected in the perpetual. The last entry on the perpetual inventory sheet should correspond to the actual amount of product on the liquor room shelf.

Since the perpetual inventory so clearly reveals a product's depletion rate, it makes ordering liquor much more precise. Among the other benefits, the perpetual inventory system greatly assists in detecting internal theft. Should the amount of product stocked on the shelf fall below the quantity shown on the perpetual inventory, first check your math—you may have made a mistake adding or subtracting on the perpetual. Check also for any unrecorded transfers or requisitions to the bar not logged onto the perpetual. Each occurrence would explain why the amount on the shelf doesn't match the figure on the perpetual. If that doesn't resolve the discrepancy, the only remaining explanation is internal theft.

- **Bar Requisitions** — This operational form is used to record the transfer of inventory from the liquor room to a specific bar or outlet. Bartenders log onto the requisition every product emptied (a.k.a. breakage) during the course of a shift. Afterwards, a replacement bottle is issued for the products being requisitioned and the transfers are noted in the perpetual inventory system. The bar requisition form should include the date and note which bar or outlet is making the request. The form should allow the bartenders to identify the exact product name, size and quantity being requisitioned. Space needs to be provided for whoever issues the stock to note how much of each product was actually delivered (in some instances there is insufficient product on-hand to meet the requisition, in which case, the requisition is marked T.O.—"Temporarily Out") and a prompt reminder to enter the transaction into the perpetual inventory.

- **Depletion Allowance Forms** — This operational form is used to record cost information regarding product that has been depleted from inventory without a corresponding sales value.

Wasted or spilled inventory should be recorded onto the depletion allowance form, listing what was spilled, in what amount and a brief comment as to the circumstance. It should be explained to the staff that no punitive measures will be taken as a result of a notation. Waste and spillage are a cost of doing business and cannot be avoided. The intent is to assign a cost to the spilled products and factor it into the pour cost analysis. The same type of notation should be made regarding transfers of inventory from one bar to another, or to the kitchen, bakery, catering, etc. The person receiving the transferred inventory should sign or initial the form. Finally, information detailing all complimentary drinks given out should be recorded onto the depletion allowance form. A manager's signature should accompany the notation of each complimentary drink.

- **Bar Par** — Every product behind the bar needs to be stocked in sufficient quantity to meet sales demand. The bar par form facilitates maintaining the inventory at prescribed levels by indicating to the staff how much of each product should be stocked behind the bar at any time. Bar par sheets should be checked daily. They are also effective in controlling internal theft. Any product missing from the shelves or back-ups is detected quickly and the disappearance reported immediately. The products should be listed alphabetically and indicate how many of each brand should be open in the well or back bar and how many are to be kept as back-ups.

- **Physical Inventory Process** — The intent behind conducting a physical audit of the inventory is to determine the dollar value of the liquor, beer and wine inventory on-hand at a specified point in time. How frequently a physical inventory is conducted depends on your volume of business. The busier you are the more control you need to maintain over the operation, and the shorter the interval between physical inventories. There are establishments that take a physical inventory on a daily basis. The result is knowing precisely what was depleted from inventory during the previous shift. A cost is then assigned to the depleted inventory, and when divided by the sales registered for that shift an exact cost percentage can be computed. If there is a problem, the management will know about it a matter of hours after a shift and they can take appropriate measures. Compare that level of control to an operation that analyzes their cost on a monthly basis. If the bar's cost percentages have increased an entire month will have elapsed before management has an opportunity to react. In some instances this can prove costly.

SECTION II:
THEFT PREVENTION THROUGH POLICIES AND PROCEDURES

It is important to understand that management policies and procedures by themselves will not stop bartenders from stealing. For example, it should be policy that bartenders are expressly forbidden to leave the cash drawer open between transactions. That directive alone, however, will not necessarily stop bartenders from leaving the cash drawer open between transactions.

On the contrary, management policies and procedures pertaining to the bar are only effective if they are strictly enforced. In addition, they must be consistently and uniformly applied to all members of the bartending staff. Presuming that the bartenders are operating in strict compliance with the establishment's set directives invites larceny and financial strangulation.

Another important consideration regarding policies and procedures is to have the employees sign a receipt affirming that they have thoroughly read and understand the handbook material, and they will perform their duties in strict adherence to the stated directives covered. With this signed receipt, management is in a solid position to hold an employee fully accountable for any future violation of stated rules governing conduct or financial property.

Not all of the following suggestions regarding policies and procedures will conform to every beverage operation's exact circumstances. This is a matter for management to decide. An establishment's set directives must be tailored to its own particular needs and requirements.

Policy — *Bartenders Prohibited From Checking-Out Their Cash at the End of a Shift*

- In many operations, bartenders are required to check-out their register's cash drawer. This entails using the cash in the drawer to compile the bar's opening bank for the following shift, and to itemize the remaining cash proceeds onto a deposit slip. If the bartenders are stealing, the check-out process provides them with an ideal opportunity to safely take out any stolen funds secretly deposited into the register's cash drawer during the course of their shift.

  By taking this daily responsibility away from the employees, management will effectively make it more difficult, and much more risky, for bartenders to withdraw stolen proceeds from the cash register or P.O.S. They will, as a result, be forced to either pull the money out of the cash drawer during the shift or opt not to use the register as a place for their stolen funds.

Policy — *Employees Not Allowed to Drink at the Bar When Off-Duty*

- While this policy may result in the bar having a few less customers, it will also prevent the bartenders from over-pouring, undercharging, or simply giving away free drinks to their co-workers. This is a sound preventative measure, intended to reduce the natural temptation bartenders face when they are put in the position of serving alcoholic beverages to people they work with. In addition, it eliminates the possibility of the establishment's personnel becoming intoxicated at their place of employment.

Policy — *Bartenders Not Allowed to Participate in the Physical Inventory Process*

- The process of taking the bar's physical inventory is solely a management function and should therefore be conducted only by management. Bartenders who are stealing from an operation can use their participation in the physical inventory process to alter the recorded data such that it offsets previous theft. This could be accomplished by overstating the amount of liquor inventory on hand at the end of the month. Overstating the amount of liquor on-hand during the physical inventory process will essentially have the same effect as if the theft never occurred.

Policy — *Bartenders Not Involved in Ordering, Receiving or Issuing of Liquor*

- The ordering, receiving, issuing, and storage of the establishment's liquor inventory should remain the sole responsibility of management. There is no legitimate reason for the bartending staff to be involved in any of these managerial functions. An unscrupulous bartender could cause immense operational difficulties by altering the establishment's internal inventory systems for illegitimate purposes.

Policy — *Banquet Bartenders Not Allowed Behind Main Bar*

- The intent behind maintaining two different bartending staffs, one to work catering and banquet functions, the other to work at the main bar, is to prevent banquet liquor inventory from being secretly brought behind the bar's main facility. If that were to occur, a bartender could sell the smuggled liquor, and pocket the entire amount of sales proceeds generated, all done without the operation's cost percentages being negatively affected.

Policy — *Bartenders Required to Take Pre- and Post-Shift Par Readings*

- The operation's bar par sheets will detail precisely how many bottles of each product in the liquor inventory should be behind the bar at any one point in time. The bartending staff should be required to take a physical bar par reading twice each day; once prior to the opening shift, and again at the conclusion of the night shift. The closing bar par must take into account the bottles emptied during the course of the shift. The bar par reading will conclusively reveal if all of the products in the liquor inventory are actually behind the bar in their prescribed quantities. If there is a discrepancy in the bar par reading, it must be investigated immediately, for it may indicate that a full bottle of liquor was stolen from the bar.

Policy — *Spillage and "Comp." Sheet Entries Require Managerial Approval*

- Bartenders should receive management approval prior to preparing the customer's complimentary drink. This policy is intended to stop them from claiming, after the fact, that a drink was given away with management's consent, when in reality the drink was sold and the proceeds of the sale were pocketed.

   The spillage sheet should require a manager's approval after the bartender has re-prepared the patron's drink, preventing any needless delay in getting the customer his or her replacement drink. This policy will not necessarily prevent a bartender from falsely recording a drink spilled, when in fact it was sold and the proceeds stolen. Nevertheless, this policy will make it harder for the bartending staff to defraud the establishment using the spillage sheet.

Policy — *Absolute Limit of One Transaction Per Drink Ticket*

- It should be mandated that bartenders record no more than one transaction per drink ticket. This is considered an essential beverage control. If bartenders are allowed to use one, long running drink ticket to record beverage sales, they will be in an ideal position to steal by not recording all of the drinks actually sold. It is nearly impossible for a casual observer to perceive if the bartender is properly ringing-in each and every sale using a running check. The best method to alleviate the problem of bartenders stealing unrecorded drinks is to require that they ring in each transaction on a separate drink check.

Policy — *Enforced "Void Out" Procedures*

↓

- It should be policy that management approval is first required before a bartender can void-out a drink check. In addition, it is important to stipulate that the bartenders must obtain the approval of the manager-on-duty before the transaction can be completed.

Policy — *Established Missing Drink Ticket Penalty*

↓

- It is extremely prudent to set policy that, in the event a bartender claims to have lost a drink check, there be a monetary penalty assessed. The dollar amount of the penalty is left up to the individual establishment. One thing to consider regarding the penalty, if the amount levied is not severe enough, it will not act as sufficient deterrent against a bartender writing down a drink order on a ticket, collecting the sales proceeds, pocketing the money, and destroying the check, the only tangible evidence that the sale ever occurred.

Policy — *Tip Jar Procedures*

↓

- It should be established policy that the bartender's tip jar be situated well away from the operation's cash register or P.O.S. If the tip jar is located right next to the register, it is far too easy for bartenders to divert stolen funds away from the register and into the tip jar. In addition, bartenders should be prohibited from making change out of their tip jar or taking currency from the tip jar and exchanging it for larger denominations out the cash drawer. If the bartenders are stealing from the business and using the cash drawer for the stolen funds, they can easily retrieve the money from the register under the pretense of making change. For example, a bartender could take five one dollar bills out of the tip jar, deposit the currency into the register, but instead of taking out a five dollar bill in exchange, remove a ten dollar bill (five dollars of which are stolen funds).

Policy — *Bartenders Prohibited From Serving Beverages to Service Staff*

- The intent behind this policy of not permitting bartenders to serve beverages to other personnel is to prevent them from giving employees alcohol. Food servers and cocktail servers can easily obtain coffee, iced tea, and water to drink from the kitchen or server stations. If the bartenders are not allowed to give other employees any beverages over the bar, it will be much more difficult for employees to drink alcohol while on-duty.

Policy — *Manager-on-Duty to Initial All Employee Time Cards*

- It should be policy that the manager-on-duty must initial all employee time cards when they clock out at the end of their shift. This practice is designed to discourage employee theft through time clock fraud.

Policy — *P.O.S. and Cash Register Procedures*

- **Strictly Enforced "No Sale" Policy** — The only acceptable use of the P.O.S. or cash register's "no sale" function is to facilitate the process of making change for a customer, in which case, the bartender must deposit money into the drawer and withdraw the exact (same) amount of change.

- **Ring-in Drink Sale Prior to Service** — Bartenders should be required to ring-in a drink sale into the cash register prior to serving it to the patron. This policy alone will make it much more difficult for the bartending staff to steal through unrecorded sales.

- **Cash Drawer Count Verification** — Bartenders should be required to verify the amount of money used to comprise the bar register's opening bank. This practice will prevent the bartenders from claiming that their opening bank was either over or under the prescribed dollar amount to explain a cash shortage or overage in the register.

On a periodic basis, place an extra ten dollar bill in the bartender's bank and see if the person informs you of the cash overage. It is a good way to verify if the bartender is counting his bank prior to the shift, as well as providing insight into the person's degree of integrity.

- **Cash Drawer Closed Between Transactions** — One of the most fundamental of all cash controls is to require that the register's cash drawer remain closed between transactions. If this is not strictly enforced, and the drawer is allowed to remain open, the primary control factor of the cash register is lost.

- **Bartenders Not Allowed to Use "Make-Up" Rings to Correct Errors** — An example of a "make-up ring" is when a bartender incorrectly inputs a $2.50 drink sale as $2.00. To correct the error, another $.50 is rung into the cash register. This technique can be easily manipulated by a bartender for fraudulent purposes and therefore should not be allowed.

- **All Transactions Must Be Rung Into Proper Sales Categories** — This policy is intended to stop bartenders from ringing soft drinks and draft beers into the liquor sales key to offset previous theft.

- **Safeguard All P.O.S. Passwords** — Ensure that all management passwords are kept safe and secure from the bartenders. This will prevent bartenders from being able to open reports and learn what their shift sales are.

Policy — *Cash Control Procedures*

- **Multiple Collections** — While it is extremely difficult and inadvisable to prohibit bartenders from collecting money from more than one customer at a time, management should stress that bartenders limit multiple collections to only the most demanding of circumstances.

- **Bartender's Required to "Fan" a Patron's Change** — Requiring bartenders to fan out a patron's change will make it much more difficult for them to short change customers. In addition, bartenders should vocalize how much change is being returned to the patron.

- **Bartender's Required to State Price of the Drink and Amount Tendered** — Bartenders should be required to state to the patron the price of the drink and verbally confirm the amount of money tendered ("That will be $2.50 out of $5.00"). This policy makes it more difficult for the bartenders to defraud the clientele through over-charging or short-changing.

Policy — *Credit Card Procedures*

- **Employees Required to Obtain Approval Codes on All Credit Cards** — Once an approval code has been obtained and recorded onto the sales voucher, the issuing bank has authorized that the credit card is authentic and that the transaction will be honored. This should be done on all credit card transactions regardless of the amount. Also, the bartender's initials should appear on the voucher as means of identification.

Policy — *Drink Pouring Procedures*

- **Bartenders Not Allowed to "Tail" Measurements** — "Tailing" is the practice of letting a bottle continue to pour after the true measure has been reached. Tailing is often used deliberately over-pour the liquor portion used in a drink, and should be prohibited.

- **No Over-Pouring or Under-Pouring Liquor Portions Allowed** — Bartenders should be expressly forbidden from purposely over-pouring or under-pouring the liquor portion in a customer's drink. Likewise, bartenders should be directed not to "top-pour" liquor or "ghost" the alcoholic portion in a blended drink. Both of these techniques are used by bartenders to steal by under-pouring the alcohol in a series of drinks.

- **Standardized Drink Recipes** — Provide the bartending staff with a comprehensive set of standardized drink recipes. It is absolutely fundamental in the pursuit of consistency of product and controlling the beverage operation's liquor costs. It should be a matter of policy that bartenders be required to pour only the drink recipes provided by management. This directive will, for the most part, prevent bartenders from over-pouring the alcoholic portion in drinks.

Policy — *Drink Tab Procedures*

- **Drink Tabs Secured by Major Credit Card** — If a customer wants to run a drink tab, the bartender should first obtain a major credit card from the customer as a type of security deposit. This practice will ensure that the establishment will receive payment in the event the customer walks out without first clearing his or her tab. If the patron does skip out on the tab, the credit card voucher should be filled out, the manager-on-duty only has to write "signature on file" where the customer would have signed, and the sales draft can be submitted to the bank for collection. If the customer pays the tab with cash, the bartender should be required to destroy the imprinted credit card voucher in view of the customer.

  Another reason to institute this policy is to prevent the bartender and customer from working together to defraud the establishment. This could be accomplished by the bartender claiming that the patron left without clearing his or her tab, when in fact, the person gave the bartender a sizable cash gratuity to let him or her leave without paying the tab amount.

- **Bartender Required to Record All Transactions on Drink Tab** — Prior to serving a patron another round of drinks, a bartender should be instructed to first record the transaction on a customer's running drink ticket. This policy is intended to make it more difficult for bartenders to steal by giving away unrecorded drinks. In addition, this policy will make it harder for bartenders to overcharge customers by ringing in a bogus round of drinks onto the running charge.

Policy — *Promotional Material Procedures*

↓

- Management must institute procedures governing the proper use of promotional material, such as chits or drink coupons. Bartenders should be provided with a set procedure to properly deal with promotional devices so that they are prevented from reusing chits or drink coupons for fraudulent purposes.

SECTION III:
THEFT PREVENTION THROUGH PROACTIVE MANAGEMENT

Attempting to prevent internal theft through set policies alone is too passive an action to stop such a challenging operational problem. There are more dynamic measures management can use in addition to the aforementioned policies and procedures to curb employee theft.

One of the crucial elements in the strategy to reduce internal theft is increasing management's physical presence in the bar. Direct observation is the best method of preventing bartenders from stealing and no one is in a better position to observe than the manager-on-duty. If an individual is trained to spot specific improprieties and is well versed in the operation's prices, policies and procedures, he or she will be ideally situated to monitor the bartenders' conduct while on-duty.

One costly misconception many managers possess is that the bar is somehow the bartenders' private domain and any managerial encroachment into their inner sanctum is intrusive and operationally disruptive. The fact that the bar facility itself often provides bartenders with the privacy and sanctuary necessary to steal warrants that managers need to occasionally intrude into that space. From such a vantage point, it is far easier for a manager-on-duty to detect evidence of internal theft.

When bartenders steal, they need to keep an accurate record of exactly how much money they have stashed in the register's drawer. If a bartender makes a mistake, the cash count and the register reading will not balance and it becomes incriminating.

Anything that could possibly be used as a record keeping system should immediately be suspect. Items such as coins, matches, sword picks, or any small, object could be used as a token. Tokens are used like poker chips to keep a tally of the amount of money the register's drawer is over. Some bartenders use a written record which they keep in their pocket or in a drawer. Some have even used the overhead glass racks and the number of glasses in each row as a make-shift abacus to track how much in stolen funds were deposited into the register. Anything closely resembling a counting scheme should be immediately investigated.

Other tell-tale signs of internal theft include an unusual number of "no sale" rings in an evening and the tip jar being inexplicably stuffed to capacity. Another clue would be the cash drawer not being normally maintained. Segregated monies might be hastily deposited proceeds of theft.

More than likely, the manager-on-duty's presence in and around the bar will have an impact on limiting internal theft. Having a manager hovering about the bar will undoubtedly act as a deterrent.

The material in this section of the chapter details numerous specific steps which management can use to exert greater control over the actions of the bartending staff and thereby lessen the beverage operation's vulnerability to internal theft.

MID-SHIFT "Z" READINGS

If a bartender is suspected of stealing and using the cash register's drawer as a place for stolen funds, the manager-on-duty can either confirm or deny those suspicions by taking a mid-shift "Z" reading of the register. At some point in the shift, the manager-on-duty should clear the register by taking a "Z" reading and replace the cash drawer in the machine with a new, fresh one. If the bartender has deposited unaccounted for funds in to the register for safe keeping, the cash drawer count will be "over" when compared to the cash register's sales totals. If the bartender starts the shift by pocketing a certain amount of money out of the cash drawer, intending to replace the money with stolen funds throughout the course of the evening, the results of the mid-shift "Z" reading will be that the register's cash drawer count will be "under" by the amount yet to be replaced.

One important element of the strategy is to periodically conduct two mid-shift readings during the course of a night. This will prevent you from being predictable. The bartenders will never be certain which nights you'll take two readings, making it riskier to use the cash drawer for stolen proceeds.

MAINTAINING A SEPARATE SOURCE FOR MAKING CHANGE

One proven technique to deterring theft through use of the "no sale" key is to provide the bartenders with an alternative source for making change. A small, inexpensive container, or even a cabinet drawer will suffice. By providing a separate source for making change behind the bar, the bartenders will no longer have a legitimate reason for accessing the cash drawer with the "no sale" key every time someone needs change. This will make it slightly more challenging to steal unrecorded sales and depositing the funds in the cash drawer without entering any sales data.

IMPLEMENTING CASH CONTROLS

- **A** — At the conclusion of "last call" the manager-on-duty should immediately take the "Z" reading of the register and pull the cash drawer out of the machine. If the bartenders are stealing and using the cash register drawer for stolen funds, this procedure will force them to withdraw the money during the shift while there are still people milling about instead of the relative privacy of closing.

- **B** — Bartenders should not have access to the cash register's keys. Only management should be able to run an "X" and "Z" reading of the register. It is a good idea to provide the bartending staff with the key which turns the register on and off. Then, if a bartender needs to leave the register unattended for a brief period of time, the machine can be turned off and the key removed, preventing the cash drawer from being opened.

- **C** — Bartenders should not be allowed to pull their charged tips from the cash register's drawer. Management should be responsible for the bartenders receiving their gratuities charged on credit cards. This policy will eliminate just one more reason for employees to take money out of the cash register and deposit it into the bar's tip jar.

- **D** — It is a very good idea to have the cash register's display facing the public portion of the bar. This will permit anyone interested enough to verify what a bartender is ringing into the cash register.

BAR STAFF NOT PRIVY TO THE OPERATION'S POUR COSTS

There are several reasons why management shouldn't inform the bartending staff of what the liquor, beer, and wine cost percentages are. If the bartending staff knows that the bar's liquor pour cost is 18%, for example, they may become ambivalent about the cost of the liquor inventory, which over time will surely drive the liquor costs upward. Another possible reaction is for the bartenders to become resentful and begrudge the operation its profits. If the bartending staff knows that the business is making 82 cents on each dollar of liquor sales, they may want to claim some of the profit margin for themselves.

USE OF A DROP BOX

One of the best methods to reduce theft through the reuse of drink tickets is to use a drop box. This device is a lockable box with a slot in the top large enough to deposit a drink ticket through. Once a ticket has been rung into the cash register and the sales proceeds collected, the bartender should be required to deposit the drink ticket into the drop box, preventing its fraudulent reuse. Any bartender caught with a previously rung in drink check should be suspect.

BOTTLE TAGGING

For establishments with more than one outlet, bottle tagging will make it possible for management to identify each issue bottle of liquor inventory. This is important to prevent employees from smuggling bottles of liquor into the operation and selling the contents to the clientele. Management must diligently check the tags affixed to the liquor bottles to ensure that they are not being wrongfully removed and reused, or that the inventory issued to one outlet doesn't show up at another of the bars.

DRINK TICKET LEDGER MAINTAINED

Management should routinely log the serial numbers of the drink checks issued to the bar prior to each shift. When the bartenders turn in their paperwork at the end of the shift, the ledger should be checked to make sure all of the drink tickets issued to the bar are present and accounted for, whether they are used or not. If this ledger is maintained, management will be in a position to determine if any of the bar's drink tickets are missing, and if so, begin the process of investigating its disappearance. A missing drink ticket should be treated as a serious, and potentially costly breach of the operation's stated policies and procedures.

USE OF MIRRORS AND TRACK LIGHTING

One physical alteration to the facility which will enhance a manager's ability to detect theft is to increase the amount of lighting behind the bar. Track lights are very effective in throwing light on previously dark and secretive areas. Mirrors are not only decorative and closely associated with bars, but they also provide managers with a number of angles to view the area.

HIDDEN VIDEO CAMERAS

A more extreme measure of control is to install a hidden remote video camera to monitor the activities behind the bar. Great care must be taken to conceal the device, for if the bartenders find out they are under constant surveillance, the staff resentment could make this tactic counterproductive. This is a very capital intensive measure, not only from a cost standpoint, but also considering the amount of management time necessary to monitor the video tapes.

HYDROMETERS

If it is suspected that the bartender might be watering down the liquor inventory, a hydrometer will either confirm or deny those suspicions. It is a device which measures the relative alcoholic content of a liquor, and since the addition of water into the liquor will naturally lower its alcoholic content, a hydrometer will indicate if the particular product in question has been tampered with.

SPOTTING OR SHOPPING SERVICES

Another option available to management is to enlist the services of a professional spotting or shopping service to scrutinize the operation. Spotters are essentially plain clothes detectives who, armed with the operation's prices, policies, and procedures, will sit at the bar for hours per visit sipping their drinks, observing the bartenders' activities. Great care must be taken when selecting which service to retain as there is a wide disparity in their professional abilities. In addition, bartenders often have a feeling that they are being watched and they will naturally curtail their clandestine activities. In that event, the detectives would submit a clean and misleading report, when in fact, the bartenders might very well be engaged in stealing from the establishment. The opposite is also possible. A spotter could misconstrue what he or she observed and report back to management that the bartenders were engaged in theft, when in reality, they were not.

In any event, management should take every conceivable step to control the problem in-house before an outside security specialist is called in.

LIQUOR PORTIONING GUIDELINES AND TECHNIQUES

There are only four methods which a bartender can use to dispense alcohol at a commercial bar. Management must weigh the advantages and disadvantages of each technique to determine which is best suited for the particular needs and requirements of the beverage operation. Each of the four different methods will have a profound impact on management's attempt to prevent bartenders from stealing liquor inventory.

The following is intended to detail the advantages and disadvantages of the various pouring techniques as they pertain to controlling internal theft.

Hand-Held Measuring Devices

- **Advantages** — Besides being able to pour virtually any measurement, the primary benefit derived by having bartenders hand-measure liquor is that all parties concerned can see precisely how much of a product is being poured. Hand-measuring can be abused for fraudulent purposes, but the bartender always runs the risk of someone, be it the customer or manager, observing exactly what was poured, which is a viable beverage control in its own right. Hand-measuring is easily trained, involves very little capital investment, and can be used to dispense any product in the liquor inventory.
- **Disadvantages** — The principle disadvantage of allowing bartenders to dispense alcohol using hand-held measuring devices is that, regardless of the fact that someone can observe what is being poured, the employee can still easily steal using this technique. In addition, some measuring devices are much better at preventing fraudulent practices than others.

For instance, the traditional two-sided stainless steel jiggers are undoubtedly the worst choice with regards to stopping internal theft. Their primary shortcomings are that they are opaque and therefore, the bartender can easily steal using these jiggers by under-pouring liquor portions. These devices are also produced in a wide variety of measurements, all of which look virtually indistinguishable from one another. A bartender could secretly switch measures, under-pour or over-pour liquor portions all evening, replace the jigger before leaving, and no one would be the wiser.

Perhaps the best hand-held measuring device, certainly the hardest to steal with, is a clear, plastic measure with between four and six measurements. These plastic jiggers are transparent, unbreakable, and very fast to use.

Bottle-Attached Measuring Devices

- **Advantages** — When functioning properly, bottle-attached devices will dispense consistent, accurate measurements. While it is not very challenging for bartenders to learn how to work around these devices, it is extremely difficult for a bartender to do it without being obvious and suspicious.

- **Disadvantages** — These devices offer no assurance that the bartenders will not over-pour or under-pour liquor. These items can be manipulated such that, by holding the bottle at an acute angle, a bartender can pour virtually any amount of liquor through the device, negating their control function. Bottle-attached measures are relatively expensive and inflexible, in as much as they are designed to dispense only one measurement.

Free-Pouring

- **Advantages** — Free-pouring is a technique of dispensing liquor without the use of a measuring device. It is the fastest of the hand-held techniques. In addition, it is a flexible method of pouring, and requires absolutely no capital expenditure to implement. Bartenders enjoy free-pouring partially because it is very stylish and graceful. Yet, from the perspective of stopping internal theft, free-pouring offers no advantages.

- **Disadvantages** — On an ongoing basis, free-pouring is perhaps the costliest method of dispensing alcohol. It is extremely easy for bartenders to, either purposely or by mistake, over-pour or under-pour the liquor portion in a drink. To compound the problem, it is very difficult for a customer or manager to observe and accurately assess how much of a product the bartender is free-pouring. These two factors combine to make free-pouring the weakest technique in the effort to prevent stealing. In addition, this method of pouring requires staff training and consistency of product is difficult to attain when the bartenders free-pour all measurements.

Electronic Liquor Dispensers

- **Advantages** — These devices are capable of dispensing liquor extremely fast and accurately. Electronic liquor dispensers (ELDs) offer some flexibility with respect to the amount of measurements which can be poured through the device. In addition, ELDs are metered so management can accurately determine how much liquor was dispensed through the device during the shift. The liquor fed into the system is stored at a secure, remote location in the facility, free from tampering. ELDs can also be tied into the beverage operation's electronic cash register, so that whenever a measure of liquor is dispensed the appropriate sales figure is automatically rung in the machine, dramatically reducing theft of unrecorded drinks and overcharging/undercharging schemes. Essentially, electronic liquor dispensers make it very difficult to steal any of the products used in the system.
- **Disadvantages** — Disregarding the fact that ELDs are capital intensive and occasionally mechanically unreliable, they cannot reasonably guarantee that bartenders will not steal using the device. Management must diligently keep track of the ELDs meter to precisely calculate each shift's liquor usage, otherwise, the meter is a useless feature. Bartenders have been known to steal by poking a hole in the ELDs liquor feed lines so that they can bleed off inventory before it is registered on the device's meter. They then have only to tape up the feed line, sell the unrecorded liquor, and pocket the stolen proceeds. A simple method is for a bartender

to dispense four measures of liquor inventory from the ELD and sell five, under-portioned mixed drinks using that pilfered alcohol. Even easier, the bartender can sell an unrecorded drink and simply assume that no one in management will notice the overage on the ELDs meter.

Another weakness in the reliance to prevent theft is that only a limited amount of product can be dispensed through the system. The remainder of the beverage operation's name brand liquors would have to be poured using one of the aforementioned techniques, thereby leaving the establishment vulnerable to theft of those products.

SCREENING PROSPECTIVE EMPLOYEES

One of the more important steps management can take to prevent employee theft is to carefully screen potential employees before they are hired. Management should certainly contact a bartender's references and check their places of previous employment. Often, past employers will gladly share valuable insights into an applicant's personality and character. When speaking with a person's previous employer, the manager should inquire under what circumstances the employee left the establishment and whether the previous employer would hire the individual again.

Attempting to gain as much insight and information about an applicant before he or she is hired is a very viable means of avoiding the many aforementioned internal problems. It is highly advisable for a prospective employee to be interviewed more than once by more than one manager. The individual should be asked difficult, probing questions and the managers should gauge their responses for themselves.

TOP TEN INDICATORS YOU'RE GETTING RIPPED OFF

1 — Low bartender productivity

2 — Spike in pour cost percentages

3 — Unusual purchasing or requisition rate

4 — Drop in anticipated gross sales

5 — Unusually high tips

6 — Comments from customers about drink strength

7 — Counting systems by the cash register

8 — "Over or under" cash drawer counts

9 — Heavy-handed "comp'ing"

10 — Two-way tip jar transactions

Chapter 4

HOW OTHER
EMPLOYEES STEAL

Whenever internal theft in the food and beverage industry is the topic of discussion, bartender theft quite naturally dominates the conversation. Nevertheless, they are not the only employees who are in a position to steal cash and inventory. This chapter will concentrate on detailing the practices these other employees use to defraud your establishment and clientele.

Cocktail servers have at their disposal almost as many methods to steal from your operation and guests as bartenders do. They enjoy nearly the same level of autonomy as their co-workers behind the bar. Since most of these servers operate well out of the range of casual observation, managers are extremely hard pressed to supervise their activities with any degree of reliable control. As a result, cocktail servers may employ an exceptionally large number of fraudulent practices.

One critical variable affecting this type of theft is whether she is acting alone or whether she has successfully enlisted the aid and assistance of the bartender-on-duty. The number of possible schemes a cocktail server can use to steal from the business and its customers increases dramatically when she and the bartender act together. These employees become a much greater threat when they act with one another.

Working alone, the bartender can only steal from the customers seated at the bar and skim from the volume of business they generate, but by working with a cocktail server, the bartender can increase both the number of clientele he can potentially defraud and the dollar amount which can be skimmed.

The cocktail server benefits by making it significantly easier in all respects to steal. By working with the bartender, the server is released from having to use deception to steal relatively small sums of money and is free to steal without any significant obstacles. At the end of the shift, the stolen proceeds can be divided up equitably and passed along to the bartender, usually in the way of a significantly increased tip-out.

The following material will detail many of the practices and schemes cocktail servers can use to steal from you and your clientele. The material is divided into two sections: the first details the scams a cocktail server can use when acting alone; the second section examines the additional opportunities available when the server and bartender conspire together.

SECTION I:
HOW COCKTAIL SERVERS
STEAL WORKING ALONE

Short-Changing — Most employees in this business understand that as alcohol begins to take its affect, most customers become less attentive to the amount of change returned to them over the course of an evening. This creates an ideal opportunity for a cocktail server to add to her tips through short-changing the clientele.

> *While short-changing will have no affect on the bar's cost percentages, it does defraud the establishment's clientele.*

Overcharging — Cocktail servers can use various overcharging techniques. For instance, they can charge customers inflated prices for their drink orders, tender the actual sales amounts to the bartender, and pocket the cash difference.

Cocktail servers are also in an ideal position to use "buck boosting". Without showing the customer the drink check, the guest is quoted a higher price for the drink order than was actually rung on the ticket. If the patron requests to see the drink check and notices the discrepancy, the server can claim that she misread the ticket and apologize for the error. If the patron goes ahead and pays the inflated total, the cash difference can be secretly pocketed.

Finally, cocktail servers can add bogus purchases to a guest's drink tab in an effort to increase the running tab's dollar total. Servers are traditionally tipped out based on the total sale, and therefore, stand to receive a better gratuity. In addition, this scheme inflates their gross sales for the night and possibly offsets previous theft.

Overcharging will not negatively impact the operation's cost percentages, but it obviously will adversely affect the establishment's clientele.

Substitutions — Cocktail servers are perhaps in a better position to use substitution scams than bartenders. Their customers are usually not able to directly observe the substitution being committed. One example of how a server can use substitutions to her benefit is when a customer orders a mixed drink made with a premium liquor, she can order the drink from the bartender specifying a well liquor instead of the premium liquor the customer actually requested. The server then delivers the drink, collects the proceeds for a premium sale, and tenders a lesser amount of money to the bartender to cover the well liquor sale. The cash difference between the premium and well drink price can then be pocketed by the server.

Substitutions will not negatively affect the bar's cost percentages, but they do victimize the establishment's clientele.

The "Looking the Other Way" Fee — This illicit, potentially legally damaging practice involves a cocktail server accepting a cash offering or incentive to serve alcohol to someone who is under the legal drinking age, or to someone who is already intoxicated. Both of these acts are expressly illegal and can result in the establishment's liquor license being revoked or suspended.

Nevertheless, the fact that they are placing the entire operation in jeopardy is sometimes insufficient to dissuade the employee from taking the cash and serving the person alcohol.

This practice will not affect the operation's cost percentages, but most assuredly will have long-term legal ramifications.

Misuse of Promotional Material — A cocktail server can illegally benefit from an establishment's attempts to generate new business through promotional devices which are redeemed by patrons for free drinks. These promotional items are typically easy to get by the employees as there are seldom any operational controls applied to their use. As a result, a cocktail server could serve a drink to a customer, collect the sales proceeds, and tender a chit to cover the purchase of the drink, allowing the server to pocket the cash proceeds.

This type of fraud will not negatively impact the bar's cost percentages.

Altered Drink Tickets — Handwritten drink tickets can be altered such that the sum of money the customer pays is higher than the total proceeds the cocktail server submits to the bartender at the end of the shift. Any successful attempt to alter the check, through erasure, cross-outs or changes after the customer has tendered money to cover the check total will allow the employee to pocket the cash difference created.

Altering drink tickets and lowering sales totals will negatively impact the beverage operation's cost percentages.

Spillage and "Comp." Drink Fraud — Spillage and waste are unavoidable. It can legitimately be caused by numerous sources. Cocktail servers can use this fact to their advantage by claiming that a drink was accidentally spilled and needs to be replaced. In reality, the server collected money for the drink she claimed was spilled. When the bartender prepares the drink again, the cocktail server has an unrecorded drink which she can give away or sell if the opportunity presents itself.

The "comp" drink sheet is an operational form used to track the cost of the complimentary drinks given away to the clientele over a specified inventory period. Cocktail servers can abuse the system to off-set the theft of unrecorded drinks. For example, a server approaches the manager-on-duty seeking approval to "comp." two guests a round of drinks. The manager agrees and signs the "comp." drink sheet. When the couple orders another round, the cocktail servers serves the drinks and pockets the cash, safe in the knowledge that the drinks have already been accounted for and that pour cost will not be affected.

Because spillage, waste and "comp" drinks are factored into the bar's cost percentages, these scams will not negatively affect the operation's pour cost.

Fake Walk-Outs — Customers skipping out on their drink or food tabs is a regrettable fact of life. Typically the establishment absorbs the loss and the cocktail server is reminded to be more attentive to the guests. The server can take advantage of the situation by collecting cash for a party's drink tab, and after the group has left, claim to the manager that the guests left without clearing out their tab. There's nothing that the manager can do about the situation at that point, and the bartender is free to pocket the cash.

Fake walk-outs will negatively affect the beverage operation's cost percentages.

Time Clock Abuse — Cocktail servers, like other employees working for your business, are capable of stealing from you using a technique called "riding the clock". This technique entails the server staying on-duty longer than necessary, adding additional payroll hours and inflating payroll expenditures.

Time clock abuse will not have any affect on the beverage operation's cost percentages.

SECTION II:
HOW COCKTAIL SERVERS STEAL
WORKING WITH BARTENDERS

As previously mentioned in this chapter, the number of fraudulent practices a cocktail server can use increases dramatically when she conspires with the bartender-on-duty. In addition to the methods and schemes detailed in Section I, cocktail servers can also use the following practices:

Reuse of Drink Tickets — With the bartender's assistance a cocktail server is able to dishonestly re-use drink tickets. The cocktail server can place a drink order with the bartender without first producing a legitimate ticket for the drinks received. The server can serve the drink order, show a previously rung ticket which corresponds to the number of drinks ordered and shows the correct prices and total. The patron, suspecting nothing, pays the server the amount due, and since the items sold were never recorded, the two employees can safely split the stolen proceeds.

> *Reuse of drink tickets will negatively impact the beverage operation's cost percentages.*

Unrecorded Sales — Once the cooperative effort between the bartender-on-duty and cocktail server is established, the server can take full advantage of the numerous schemes involving the theft of unrecorded sales. For instance, a cocktail server can obtain mixed drinks from the bartender without first recording the transaction onto a drink ticket. Since there is no record of the sale, the cocktail server can deliver the drinks, collect the proceeds, and at a later time, the two employees can divide the stolen cash.

This also provides an opportunity to steal by giving away unrecorded drinks in exchange for better cash tips. The same result can be obtained when a cocktail server delivers a round of drinks to a table and purposely doesn't add the items to the patron's running tab. The server will coyly let it be known that the drinks are free, compliments of the bartender and herself.

A variation of selling unrecorded drinks involves the cocktail server going up to the bar and placing a drink order, but instead of giving the bartender a properly written ticket for the transaction, she puts up a previously rung guest check. The bartender makes the requested drinks and goes through the motion of red-lining the ticket as if it were legitimate. To anyone watching, it all looks entirely appropriate. The cocktail server will then deliver the drinks, collect the proceeds, and when safe to do so, split the funds with the bartender. Another technique designed to achieve the same end entails the cocktail server delivering what will be the final round sold to a table, collecting the proceeds for the order, and pocketing the cash. When the people leave, she and the bartender ask the manager-on-duty to void their guest check, explaining that the customers changed their minds and canceled the order before the drinks had actually been prepared. The manager, noting nothing particularly suspicious, voids the drink ticket, allowing the two employees to split the stolen cash at a later time.

Giving away free drinks and selling unrecorded drinks will negatively impact the beverage operation's cost percentages.

Over-Pouring — In an attempt to increase the likelihood of receiving a better tip, the cocktail server can request the bartender to over-pour the liquor portion in the guest's drink. In reality, the only things which are sure to increase by over-pouring the alcoholic portion in the patron's drink are the operation's cost percentages and the rate the individual will become intoxicated.

Over-pouring liquor will negatively impact the beverage operation's cost percentages.

Drinking On-Duty — This last method of theft involves the cocktail server obtaining alcohol from the bartender and drinking while still on-duty. You not only lose the cost of the inventory the server personally consumed, but, as the alcohol begins to negatively affect the server's abilities, you are also out competent help in the cocktail lounge.

Drinking on-duty will negatively impact the beverage operation's cost percentages.

SECTION III:
HOW FOOD SERVERS STEAL

Waiters and servers must first enlist the aid and cooperation of the bartender-on-duty before they can successfully steal from the bar on anything more than a sporadic basis. It is improbable at best, to think a food server could defraud an establishment without the bartender being aware of it. How could a server obtain a mixed drink without presenting the bartender with either a bona fide guest check or cash proceeds without the bartender being aware of the fraud?

There's an old ploy in which a waiter acts frenzied and rushed, blurts out an order, grabs the drinks as they're prepared, and dashes off promising the bartender that he'll bring back the guest check just as soon as possible. Of course, an appropriate time never seems to arrive.

Yet, even in that scenario, the bartender is aware of the fact that liquor was given out to that server without a sale. If, as it turns out, the bartender allows the server to get away with it, regardless of the reason, he or she is an accomplice to whatever became of the unrecorded drink order.

In almost every case where a food server is stealing from the bar, the bartender-on-duty is inevitably involved. The following details some possible schemes and practices food servers can use to steal when assisted in this manner.

Overcharging/Undercharging — With the bartender's approval, food servers are free to overcharge or undercharge the clientele on purchases from the bar. A waiter or server can benefit from overcharging a customer for their drinks by inflating the total amount due on the guest check at the end of the evening. Traditionally, servers are tipped on a percentage of the total dollar amount of the guest's check. By artificially increasing the total amount the customer is charged, the server stands to receive a better gratuity.

Undercharging guests for their drinks can only result in the waiter or server being favored by the guest. In return, these employees fully expect to be repaid in kind with a better gratuity.

Overcharging guests for their drinks will cause bar's pour costs to drop, while undercharging will negatively impact the cost percentages.

Drinking On-Duty — Without exception, employee should never be permitted to consume alcohol while on-duty. It not only steals your liquor inventory, but also deprives the business of sober, competent help. Regardless, when a bartender is working with food server(s), there is little if any resistance offered to giving out alcoholic beverages to waiters and servers while they are still on-duty. In addition to the positive social implications, bartenders often give out alcohol to food servers in exchange for a slightly better tip at the end of the shift.

Drinking on-duty will negatively impact the beverage operation's cost percentages.

Adding Bogus Sales — With the bartender's assistance, food servers can add bogus drink purchases to a customer's guest check. This is done, once again, in an effort to inflate the customer's bill and to hopefully increase the amount of gratuity. Many waiters and servers believe that few patrons, take the time to verify the beverage charges on the back of the guest check. The large majority of customers gloss over it or accept the dollar amount of their bar tab as accurate. This disinterest creates an ideal opportunity for food servers to defraud the establishment's clientele.

While defrauding the guests, adding customer's drink tabs will positively impact the beverage operation's cost percentages.

Unrecorded Sales — Once the cooperative effort between the bartender-on-duty and food server is established, the server can take full advantage of the numerous schemes involving the theft of unrecorded sales. For instance, a waiter can obtain mixed drinks from the bartender without having to first record the transaction onto a drink ticket. Since there is no record of the sale, the server can deliver the drinks to the clientele, collect the proceeds for the sales, and at a later time, the two employees can divide the stolen cash.

A variation of selling unrecorded drinks involves the waiter placing a drink order at the bar, but instead of giving the bartender a properly written ticket for the transaction, the server tenders a previously rung-in guest check. The bartender makes the requested drinks and simply goes through the motion of red-lining the ticket as if it were legitimate. To anyone watching, it all looks entirely appropriate. The waiter will then deliver the drinks, collect the proceeds, and when safe to do so, split the ill-gotten funds with the bartender.

Giving away free drinks and selling unrecorded drinks will negatively impact the beverage operation's cost percentages.

SECTION IV:
HOW MANAGERS STEAL

Middle management can be a necessary and critical element to a food and beverage operation's long-term prospects. Yet, as a result of their position of authority and unlimited access, there is perhaps no one in a more opportune situation to routinely steal cash and inventory.

In the majority of bars and restaurants, middle managers are not actively involved in day-to-day preparation and service of the operation's products, effectively eliminating most of the previously mentioned fraudulent practices they can use to steal from the business. There are, however, two major types of internal theft managers can easily pull-off on a regular basis.

Theft of Cash Receipts and Inventory — Managers are frequently given the responsibility of clearing out the cash register or P.O.S. at the end of each shift. Managers are also usually assigned the duty of preparing the bartenders' opening banks and the beverage operation's daily deposit. A dishonest manager is in a position to alter the bar's transactional information and steal cash receipts. He or she can simply take money from the bar's deposit and claim that the bartender's cash drawer was short, shifting the blame onto the employee.

A manager could also steal from a business by taking a premature "Z" reading of the cash register. For instance, with an hour of sales left in a night, a manager could clear the bar's register, offering the bartender(s) some plausible explanation for the action. At the end of the shift, the manager would take another "Z" reading of the register, showing precisely how much money had been deposited in sales during the previous hour. The manager has only to discard the second register tape, take the money deposited during the last hour of business, and no one would be the wiser.

There are several other variations of these schemes that a manager can employ. Likewise, there are an unlimited variety of ways that someone in middle management can steal the liquor inventory. The manager is usually given the responsibility of closing, placing the individual in the facility when everyone else has already departed. Stealing under those conditions is anything but an imaginative process. It involves nothing more than taking whatever products he or she wants out the door. Managers can even mask this kind of theft by altering the operation's inventory records. If the theft is discovered, there are more likely candidates who'd be considered before suspicion would fall on the manager.

Inventory Abuse — In most establishment's, managers are given the assignment of conducting the beverage operation's end-of-month physical inventory. A manager handed this task is in an ideal situation to offset any previous theft he or she may have committed by altering the raw data recorded during the process of taking the physical inventory.

For example, if the manager consistently overstates the amount of liquor inventory on hand at the end of the month, the operation's cost percentages will be positively affected and unrealistically low. This is impossible to detect once the beverage operation swings into action the next day. If the manager has been engaged in any fraudulent practices involving either the liquor inventory or the bar's gross sales, overstating the amount of liquor on hand at the end of the month will make detection of those previous thefts nearly impossible using standard cost analysis.

The theft of cash and inventory will negatively impact the beverage operation's cost percentages.

Chapter 5

DEFENDING AGAINST OTHER EMPLOYEE THEFT

SECTION I:
PREVENTING COCKTAIL SERVER THEFT

Detecting cocktail server theft is an extremely difficult assignment, one which is much more challenging in many respects than catching bartenders in the act of stealing. Bartenders are confined behind the bar, and as a result are easily observed. In addition, someone watching the bar can observe both ends of a transaction, both the ordering and preparation of a drink order, as well as the financial end of the sale.

It is not an easy task to monitor the cocktail server's activities without becoming highly conspicuous in the process. This server can be operating well away from casual observation. Also, it is very difficult for someone watching the cocktail servers to catch them stealing because only one end of a transaction can be readily seen; either someone can observe the customer in the lounge placing the drink order and the subsequent sale, or the person can see the cocktail server placing the order at the bar and receiving the drinks from the bartender. It is nearly impossible to position yourself such that you can witness both ends of the transaction without appearing obvious.

It is, therefore, important to implement specific policies and measures that are designed to curtail the fraudulent activities of cocktail servers. The following are preventative measures from which an effective strategy can be formulated to reduce the incidence of cocktail server theft.

Policy — *The Returning of Customers' Change*

↓

- When a cocktail server returns change to a customer, she must place the money on a tip tray, fanning out the bills in such a manner that the patron can easily confirm the exact amount of change being returned. Coins are to be placed on top of the currency. This type of policy is intended to reduce the incidence of servers short-changing the clientele.

Policy — *Server to Present Drink Ticket to Guest Prior to Collection*

↓

- Before a cocktail server collects the proceeds for a drink order, the customer is to be presented the guest check, confirming the actual transaction. This policy gives the patron the opportunity to review what is being charged. Presenting the customer's drink ticket prior to collection will help prevent numerous fraudulent practices.

Policy — *Applicable Promotional Material Affixed to Guest Check*

↓

- When a cocktail server accepts a drink coupon or chit from a customer, she is to affix the promotional device to the patron's drink check and mark it to prevent its reuse. The purpose behind this policy is to prevent servers from reusing drink coupons or chits to offset previous theft.

Policy — *Altered Drink Checks Require Manager's Approval*

↓

- When a cocktail server presents an altered drink ticket, it must be approved by the manager-on-duty before the end of the employee's shift. The server must explain to the manager the circumstances which required altering the guest check. The intent behind this policy is to make it harder for cocktail servers to steal by altering drink tickets. It should go without saying that cocktail servers are always to use a pen when writing drink orders onto tickets. The same policy should also apply to voiding a check.

Since servers can steal by voiding out a drink check, a manager's approval should be required before a voided ticket is accepted.

Policy — *All Server Claims of Spillage Require Manager's Approval*

- It should be a set policy that whenever a cocktail server makes the claim that a customer's drink order was accidentally spilled, the manager-on-duty be required to approve the remaking of the original order. This is meant to make it more complicated for a cocktail server to claim that a drink order was spilled, receive another set of drinks, and sell the unrecorded drinks, pocketing the cash. If a manager's approval is required, the server cannot be certain that the manager won't investigate the legitimacy of the claim.

Policy — *Cocktail Servers Need to Obtain Manager Initials on Time Card*

- In an effort to discourage employees from "riding the clock", cocktail servers should be required to obtain the manager's initials on their time cards when checking out at the end of a shift.

Policy — *No Beverages For Personal Consumption Given to Servers From the Bar*

- One of the most effective methods of preventing cocktail servers from drinking while on-duty is to prohibit them from obtaining beverages for their own consumption from the bar. They have access to coffee, iced tea, and water from either the kitchen or the server stations. There is no reason to allow employees to get beverages from over the bar, especially when those drinks may very well be laced with the operation's liquor inventory.

Policy — *Cocktail Server Drink Ordering Systems*

- There are three standard systems used for cocktail servers to order drinks from the bartender: the server can carry a cash caddy and pay the bartender for each drink order directly out of her bank; record each order onto drink tickets and use a red-line system or be required to "precheck" their orders prior to approaching the bar. Each method has its advantages and disadvantages with respect to preventing internal theft.

- **Cash (Caddy) System** — The cash caddy is a device which attaches to the cocktail server's drink tray, and holds the server's bank. When a cocktail server orders a round of drinks from the bar, she pays the bartender after they've been prepared. The server then delivers the drinks to the customers and collects the sales proceeds, depositing both the sales amount and any gratuity received into the cash caddy. At the end of the shift, the cocktail server's opening bank and sales receipts are subtracted and the remaining cash is her gratuities for the evening.

  This system does have its advantages. Paying cash for each drink received does tend to cut down on the amount of unrecorded sales, free drinks, and under-charging schemes. On the other hand, it doesn't have an affect on her ability to over-charge, use any of the substitution schemes, or short change the clientele.

  The primary disadvantage of the cash caddy system is that management does not have a hard copy of each of the cocktail server's transactions. This lack of a record is a major deficiency and leaves the beverage operation open to most every fraudulent practice a cocktail server and bartender can concoct between them.

- **Drink Tickets and the Red-Lining System** — The principle benefit of having cocktail servers use drink tickets is that they provide an accurate record of what was ordered and how much the patron was charged. At any point in time, you can reconstruct a transaction and hold the employee accountable. Drink tickets also afford the server the viable option of running an open tab for a customer. This system cuts down on the incidence of unrecorded sales, free drinks, and undercharging schemes.

Management must implement the use of drop boxes and require that the bartenders red line the drink tickets, indicating that the order was actually prepared and that the prices charged were correct. In addition, management should diligently track the serial numbers of the drink tickets issued to each cocktail server in order to prevent servers from pocketing an entire transaction, both the drink ticket and sales proceeds.

This system does have its disadvantages though. Drink tickets can be fraudulently reused, altered, or destroyed. Cocktail servers can still overcharge patrons and use the numerous substitution schemes with the bartender's complicity.

USE OF A P.O.S. SYSTEM TO "PRECHECK" COCKTAIL SERVER DRINK ORDERS

One of the best methods to disrupt any possible complicity between the cocktail servers and the bartender is to require them to "precheck" their drink orders into a p.o.s. system prior to approaching the bar. The intent behind this system is to eliminate the possibility of employees giving away free drinks, unrecorded sales, overcharging, and undercharging the clientele. The bartender should still be directed to only prepare the drink order that has been "prechecked" with a hardcopy in-hand from a remote printer located at the bar.

PRODUCTIVITY ANALYSIS FOR DETECTING COCKTAIL SERVER THEFT

Staff productivity is a viable gauge of an employee's efficiency and professional capabilities, and is often the first internal analytical measure that an employee is stealing. Productivity measures an individual's gross sales per hour. When analyzed over a period of time and compared to the other employees on staff in the same position, a manager can often perceive very revealing trends.

For example, if the cocktail staff operates with an average sales per hour of $78.00, and one of the servers on the staff consistently performs far below that figure, there are only a few possible explanations. The individual in question might simply be too slow to keep up with the sales demand, which would account for her sales per hour being below the staff average. Perhaps the cocktail server gives her customers extremely poor, inhospitable service, which would also have a marked negative effect on her sales per hour. Another explanation is that she might be scheduled on all of the slowest shifts and not have the same opportunity to generate the same sales per hour, or, she might be stealing a significant amount of her sales.

SECTION II:
PREVENTING FOOD SERVER THEFT

Food server theft is a simpler proposition than was the case with the bartenders and cocktail servers. There are primarily two reasons for this. First, food servers must ordinarily write a customer's drink order on a guest check, and the beverages are not paid for separately, they are automatically included into the total bill. This alone dramatically reduces the number of fraudulent practices at a food server's disposal. Secondly, since waiters and servers are customarily tipped a percentage of the total bill of fare, it is in the server's best interest that the customer is charged for all of the delivered products.

Yet, with the bartender's assistance, food servers may steal from the bar. The following items are designed to reduce the incidence of food server theft to an absolute minimum.

USE OF A P.O.S. SYSTEM TO
"PRECHECK" SERVER DRINK ORDERS

One of the best methods to disrupt any possible complicity between the food servers and the bartender is to require waiters and servers to "precheck" their drink orders into a p.o.s. system prior to approaching the bar. The intent behind this system is to eliminate the possibility of employees giving away free drinks, unrecorded sales, overcharging, and undercharging the clientele. The bartender should still be directed to only prepare the drink order that has been "prechecked" with a hardcopy in-hand from a remote printer located at the bar.

MANAGEMENT TO MAINTAIN LEDGER OF SERVER'S GUEST CHECK SERIAL NUMBERS

It is extremely important in the effort to prevent food server theft for management to maintain an accurate record of the serial numbers of the guest checks issued to each waiter or server. This ledger is a method of ensuring that a food server doesn't pocket a blank guest check, an action which will assuredly wind up costing the establishment money. If management does determine that an employee has "lost" a ticket, the disappearance must be vigorously investigated and the circumstances considered highly suspicious until the situation is resolved one way or another.

ALL SERVER CLAIMS OF SPILLAGE SHOULD BE INVESTIGATED

If a food server claims that a drink order was accidentally spilled, the manager-on-duty should investigate the claim before the bartender remakes the original drink order. This practice should effectively eliminate servers from defrauding an operation by claiming that products were accidentally spilled, when in reality, the drink order was delivered and the server is looking to receive some unrecorded drinks to sell or give away.

NO BEVERAGES FOR PERSONAL CONSUMPTION GIVEN TO SERVERS FROM THE BAR

The best method of preventing food servers from drinking alcohol while they are on-duty is to prohibit them from obtaining any beverage for their personal consumption from the bar. They have unlimited access to coffee, iced tea, and water from the server stations to drink while they are working.

SECTION III:
PREVENTING MANAGER THEFT

This category of employee theft is perhaps the most difficult category of internal theft to effectively prevent. No one employed by the business is in a more opportune position to steal from an operation than a manager. They have virtually unlimited access to all areas, including cash and inventory. In addition, there is no other employee who can steal with absolutely no possibility of being observed committing the crime like a manager.

There are three key managerial directives which will reduce a manager's ability to steal cash or inventory from a business.

DELEGATION OF ALL CASH HANDLING RESPONSIBILITIES AND RECONCILING REGISTER OR P.O.S. TO THE BOOKKEEPER

One of the two principle methods a manager can use to steal from a business is to take currency during the nightly process of reconciling the beverage operation's cash drawers. One measure to prevent this from occurring is to delegate the responsibility of reconciling the bar's cash register or p.o.s. system to the business's bookkeeper.

The manager-on-duty should take a "Z" reading of the bar's register or p.o.s. immediately upon the conclusion of the bartender's shift and deposit the cash from the register's drawer and the sales tape(s) into a lockable bank deposit bag or the office safe. This process should be done with the bartender present, avoiding any future allegation of impropriety and manager theft. Once the sales proceeds and accompanying paperwork are deposited into a locked bank bag or the office safe, the manager-on-duty will have no other opportunity to steal currency from the operation's cash drawer.

The daily responsibility for compiling the bartender's opening bank and the bar's bank deposit should be delegated to the (bonded) bookkeeper.

SECURING THE OPERATION'S
INVENTORY FROM MANAGER THEFT

The second method a manager can take advantage of is to steal the liquor inventory. The manager must have access to the liquor room, this for the practical reason of requisitioning the liquor to the bar. Once the business has closed for the night and no one else is in the facility, the liquor inventory, both behind the bar and in the liquor room, is especially vulnerable to internal theft.

The liquor behind the bar should be stored in lockable cabinets at the end of the night shift, effectively eliminating theft. The inventory in the liquor room is another matter. The manager has access to the liquor room, as well as the operation's perpetual inventory records. A motivated manager can make off with a sizable amount of liquor on an ongoing basis and alter the perpetual inventory records to conceal the theft.

The only practical method of preventing a manager from leaving the operation each night with a stolen bottle of liquor, or from even backing a truck up to the back door and emptying the place, is to retain the services of a security guard to watch the business at closing.

The period of time closely corresponding to closing is when the business is most vulnerable to both internal theft of this kind or armed robbery. Closing is the one time each day when there is the most money on the premises and the least amount of personnel present. A security guard can not only make it harder for an unscrupulous manager to steal inventory out the back door at closing, but the guard can also decrease the likelihood of an armed robber gaining access through the back door.

Chapter 6

LIMITING LOSSES THROUGH HUMAN RESOURCE MANAGEMENT

The material in this chapter is only meant to be used as a guide. Any company policies or questions regarding interviewing, hiring, or termination of employment should be thoroughly reviewed by an attorney before being implemented.

Up to this point, employee theft has been scrutinized from a motivational perspective, a hands-on point of view, and finally, how management can effectively reduce specific practices. Yet, there are several other aspects regarding internal theft which should be discussed. These other considerations cover a wide range of related material, all of which will have a definite impact on the continuing effort to limit internal theft.

HIRING THE BEST BARTENDERS
THE FIRST TIME AROUND

Amassing an honest, qualified bartending staff requires time and a good deal of effort. Bartenders are key employees. They serve your clientele, dole out your inventory, and have their hands in the till. Selecting the right person for the job on the first pass requires preparation and the ability to learn a lot about a person in a very short period of time.

One of the attributes effective interviewers have in common is being a good listener. It's extremely difficult to learn anything about a prospective employee if you're doing most of the talking. Watch the person's facial expressions and body language. Use every valid impression you can to help you make the right choice the first time.

The costs of hiring the wrong bartender can be staggering. It's better to operate short-handed for a period of time and rely on your existing staff to cover the bar than hiring someone unqualified or inappropriate for the establishment. It will be more advantageous in the long-run to delay hiring another bartender until the right candidate can be found.

Here are some tips on how to get better results.

- **Application Presentability** — The appearance of a person's application for employment often reveals as much about his or her level of professionalism and attention to detail as does the written information it contains. It's neatness, correctness, and presentation reflects much about the applicant. Make note of how the document looks and any impression it might give you about the person.

- **Screen for Scheduling Limitations** — When you're handed a completed application, ask the individual a few screening questions, such as how many hours a week he or she needs to work, and how much money the person needs to earn a week. Also, find out if the applicant has reliable transportation, and if there are any scheduling conflicts you should be aware of. A few, initial probing questions can often save you from making a poor hiring decision later on.

- **Check All Listed References** — Prospective bartenders should be asked to supply three or four professional references, people who can be contacted about the individual's abilities, character, and work ethic. If after the initial interview the applicant seems like a contender, take the time to contact the person's references. Failing to do so may expose you to charges of negligence at a later date. Contact references in the reverse order they are listed on the application. People will typically list references in the order they want them contacted.

- **Stated Work Experience** — Even if an applicant provides you with an accurate accounting of work experience, it may portray an incomplete picture of competency. Experience is an intangible commodity. It's important in an interview to determine how the applicant's work experience qualifies the person for the position.

- **Don't Oversell the Job** — It's best to give a realistic estimate of how many hours a week a prospective employee might work, and how much the person can expect to earn. Likewise, don't give the applicant an overly optimistic impression of his or her advancement prospects within the company. The person could become disillusioned and resentful as the reality of the situation sets in.

- **Note Your Thoughts During Interview** — Develop a form to record your impressions and observations during an interview. It should contain a list of interview questions, and a section for rating the interviewee on the various sought-after qualities and attributes. Use of a standardized form will make the interviewing process more uniform, and more likely achieve a beneficial result.

- **Eye Contact** — When conducting an interview, it's advisable to maintain steady eye contact with applicant. The eyes often reveal into the person's level of confidence, truthfulness, and character. If the person has difficulty maintaining your eye contact, it may provide some insight into his or her personality.

- **Ask Open-Ended Questions** — One key to conducting an effective interview is to ask questions that are challenging and difficult to answer without a lengthy response. Probe for the person's limitations. Ask questions that require an individual to address his or her professional strengths and weaknesses. Essentially, the more penetrating the question, the tougher it is to answer, the more you'll learn by asking it. Consider the following examples:

A. What is the worst thing your former employer could say about you? What is the best thing?
B. What would you do if you caught a fellow employee stealing from you?
C. What are your major job-related weaknesses? Strengths?
D. What do you like most about bartending? What do you like least?
E. If you could change one thing about yourself, what would it be?
F. If you could change one thing about your former manager, what would it be?

- **Personal Stability** — Considering the high cost of employee turnover, assessing a prospective bartender's personal circumstances and stability is advisable. For instance, some might consider an applicant who is married less of an employment risk than someone who is single. People who tend to stay at their job for more than a year exhibit more stability than those who move from one place to another after only a few months.

- **Conduct Two Interviews** — The hiring process is too crucial to rely on only one interview, or one set of impressions to make the hiring decision. It is optimum to have another person conduct a second interview, after which, you'll have someone to compare notes with.

- **Testing Professional Aptitude** — Before the second interview, test the applicant's knowledge of bartending. Include questions about mixology, products, and alcohol-awareness. The results of the test will give you a better idea of the person's level of expertise and, to a degree, his or her stated work experience.

- **Personality and Demeanor** — Not everyone has the personality to be a bartender. Likewise, not everyone is compatible with the existing staff. It's important to determine whether the person will fit in with your clientele, fellow-employees, and management team. The ability to remain calm, composed, and emotionally in control is an another important bartending attribute to assess.

- **Ability to Learn and Adapt** — No matter how experienced a bartender is, there will still be aspects of the employment which require the person to adapt to a new way of doing things. While you're interviewing prospective bartenders, assess how flexible and willing to learn the individual appears to be. Avoid hiring bartenders who think their learning days are behind them.

AN EMPLOYEE HANDBOOK AND ITS AFFECT ON INTERNAL THEFT

Get a new car and you get an owner's manual. Get drafted into the NBA or NFL and they'll give you a play book. Get hired as a bartender or food server and you'll likely get a handshake, three training shifts and photocopies of house policies.

Is that all you give to your employees?

And yet, employing someone is fraught with legal ramifications. Make a mistake and you could find yourself on the wrong end of a civil lawsuit or in front of the National Labor Relations Board, where nine out of ten employees leave victorious. Suits for wrongful discharge, sexual harassment and racial discrimination are among the most prevalent employment-related litigation with judgments averaging in the six-figure range.

The first line of legal defense is a comprehensive, well-structured employee handbook, one that clearly defines the employees' job descriptions, areas of responsibilities, and all of the operation's policies and procedures. Without it, legally holding employees accountable for their actions is practically impossible.

Drafting an employee handbook is similar to creating an employment contract, which is how the courts typically view the document. And like a contract, employees are typically asked to sign a statement that they have received the handbook, read it thoroughly and agree to abide by all of its provisions. There are excellent reference materials and seminars available to help you draft an employee handbook from, among others, the National Restaurant Association and the American Hotel and Motel Association.

[Note: These are general guidelines only. Employment laws and rights vary by state, and it is incumbent upon employers to ensure that company policies and practices conform to state and federal laws. Employee handbooks should be reviewed by a lawyer who specializes in employment law before they are distributed.]

While an employee handbook need not be filled with legal terms, it does need to deal with each item in a thorough and comprehensive manner. For example, it is not enough to state that sexual harassment on-the-job will not be tolerated. Define specifically what actions constitute sexual harassment. Employees should be advised as to a course of action they can follow if sexually harassed by a customer, by another employee, by a supervisor or by the owner. How they should respond will differ with each situation. Finally, you should detail what disciplinary actions will be taken in the event of sexual harassment.

The first section of an employee handbook is referred to as the "new hire packet." It contains material helpful to new employees, including a statement describing the operation's concept, a brief history of the company and specific information about the business, such as the names of the owner(s) and managers, operating hours, happy hour information, credit cards accepted, etc.

The new hire packet should also contain a job description for each position, uniform specifications for all positions, a current copy of the menu, the bar's price lists, and an explanation of all applicable kitchen and bar abbreviations. To emphasize its importance, the operation's policies and procedures concerning the service of alcohol should be covered in the first section for every employee, regardless of position, to read and be familiar with. Include a policy statement regarding the service of alcohol to minors or someone visibly intoxicated and ask employees to sign the statement affirming their intentions to uphold the policy.

The second section of the handbook covers the operation's policies and procedures beginning with the conditions of employment. For example, employment is usually considered an "at will" relationship, meaning that it is for an indefinite period of time, that either the employee or you may terminate the relationship with or without cause, without previous notice and without liability. You should also state if you are an equal opportunity employer.

Every business has general operating policies such as how soon before a shift an employee can clock-in, how employees are to report tipped income, what constitutes full-time employment, what policies govern overtime, and how much advance notice is required if an employee is sick and cannot cover a shift.

Do you allow your employees to frequent your establishment when they're not on-duty? Do you permit smoking or eating on-duty? Drinking alcohol? When can employees give customers a complimentary drink? Do you allow co-worker dating? On-the-job gambling?

After stating in the handbook how these situations, and numerous others, are to be handled, how will you respond if employees fail to comply? You must explain your company's disciplinary policies clearly. Moreover, you should list what you consider grounds for verbal reprimands or written warnings, and what their cumulative effects will be. What do you consider gross misconduct? What consequences can someone abusing alcohol or drugs on-the-job expect?

Is it company policy to make employees pay for shortages in the cash register drawer? What is your policy regarding cash overages in the drawer? What do you consider grounds for immediate termination?

The employee handbook has the potential for becoming more than just a legal document of operational policies and procedures. It presents a singular opportunity to provide employees with insight into what is expected of them as professionals and how they can best achieve those expectations.

In this final section of the book, give your staff an understanding of what their responsibilities are as employees of the company. For example, employees are generally expected to respect the confidentiality of company matters. Things they may be privy to regarding the company should be considered confidential and not repeated to others. Employees are expected to help maintain a safe working environment and report any safety-related information to management.

Is it your company's policy to periodically evaluate employee performance? If so, what factors will you use to assess their on-the-job effectiveness? Considerations for promotion and salary increases, such as job performance, work attitude, attendance record, team compatibility and safety record, should be fully explained.

Does your staff have all of the information and knowledge necessary to perform their job description to their fullest? All employees, regardless of position, should be able to competently answer customer questions regarding menu items and daily specials. Bartenders should be capable of properly serving food at the bar and food servers should be well-trained at beverage service. The staff should know what brand name products, beers and wines are stocked at the bar.

No doubt you expect your service staff to also be competent at sales, which is a learned ability. Do your employees understand their role as salesmen? Are they familiar with suggestive selling techniques? Do they understand the effectiveness of offering customers choices? Improving your staff's sales abilities will not only increase your gross sales, it will also enhance their money-making abilities.

Anything you believe is important for your staff to know regarding their job should be covered to the degree you will hold them responsible. If providing your customers with exemplary service is crucial to your operation's success, that should be clearly stated and service guidelines along with training should be provided.

Don't presume your employees know or understand anything regarding the operation of your business. Inevitably the presumption will wind up costing you. If it's important, write it down. Then personally go over the material with your employees and hold them accountable for what it says. You'll reduce the risk of misunderstanding and ultimately get a more professional, cohesive staff.

REDUCING BARTENDER TURNOVER AND
ITS AFFECT ON INTERNAL THEFT

When an operation first opens its doors to the public, the incidence of internal theft is predictably at its lowest point, and perhaps, will even be nonexistent. The question, therefore, is why should employee theft be virtually nonexistent during the initial stages of a business and only during that phase? Secondly, what transpires over time to change the situation?

One plausible explanation for why internal theft would be at its lowest point when an operation first opens for business lies in the pervasive attitude that develops within the employees and the group psychology which manifests itself during this special, one-time occurrence. When a bar or restaurant opens for business, the employees are positive, upbeat, motivated, and enthusiastic. It is a new beginning for everyone involved. People enjoy the newness, the sense of a fresh start, and the seemingly unlimited potential of the new enterprise.

It is usually during this "opening" process that the bartending staff, for example, is the most cohesive and cooperative. Everyone involved, employees and management alike, work together, combining their efforts and talents for the good of the enterprise. There is a pervasive, almost tangible, feeling of pride and accomplishment.

It only stands to reason that the incidence of employee theft would be at its absolutely lowest point during "opening". Any employee who would steal from his or her employer during this initial "honeymoon" phase is certainly the exception rather than the rule.

As time goes by, much of the enthusiasm and camaraderie exhibited during the early days of the business fades. One by one, members of the "opening crew" begin to turnover. The pervasive sense on oneness is slowly replaced by more mundane prosaic considerations, such as hours, tips, and the weekly schedule. Eventually, most employees begin to adopt an "out-for-number-one" attitude. These are the conditions under which internal theft thrives.

One effective means of deterring this erosion of attitude is for management to create a positive work environment, and to understand that employee turnover is costly and detrimental to the overall welfare of the business. It is in management's best interest to make every attempt within reason to ensure that employee turnover is kept to an absolute minimum. If accomplished, it will have a pronounced, positive effect on limiting employee theft.

REDUCING BARTENDER TURNOVER

When a bartender resigns from a bar or restaurant's staff, the person's departure weakens the business. It may not be appreciated at the time, but invariably, when an experienced employee in a skill position leaves a service-oriented business, the enterprise will suffer as a result. There is a high-cost associated with bartender turnover.

When a bartender leaves the staff, your beverage operation loses all of the on-the-job training you've invested in the employee, as well as, all of the expertise and experience the individual was able to accrue at the position. You must begin the selection process anew; applications, interviews, paperwork, training shifts, and then, at the end of the process, the operation must suffer with the new employee's inefficiency. In addition, the rest of your bartending staff will have to compensate for the new bartender's inability's. There will be scheduling changes required as the new bartender most likely will not be capable of working the busier shifts.

These costs do not take into consideration the increase in management supervision necessary to ensure the employee is adequately trained. It is also reasonable to assume that the bartender's departure will negatively impact staff morale, customers' perceptions and gross sales. Suffice it to say, bartender turnover is a costly occurrence, certainly something to be avoided whenever possible.

One key element in the process of reducing turnover behind the bar is to make a concerted effort to hire the most stable, capable and mature bartenders as the situation permits. There is little that can be done if there isn't an emotionally stable, well-intentioned bartending staff already in place.

Of equal or greater importance is creating a positive working environment. Negative pressures and stress can be cumulative in effect and cause a deterioration of staff attitude and professionalism. This inevitably leads to a drop in proficiency, burnout and turnover. When bartenders and servers stop caring about their performance on the job their customer are the first to suffer, followed closely by the operation as a whole. Without a proper attitude, a bartender's productivity can be expected to drop and liquor cost, spillage and waste to increase.

Creating a positive working environment is essential in reducing turnover and requires managers to use restraint, patience and fairness when dealing with their employees. The following are some suggestions on how to reduce bartender turnover while creating a positive working environment:

- **Keep the Bartending Staff Challenged** — Professionalism is an ambitious objective, one not easily achieved. Instill within your staff a sense of craftsmanship and a desire to excel. Continually challenging your bartenders is motivating and will help to stave off on-the-job "burnout."

- **Solicit the Bartending Staff's Feedback** — Bartenders are the resident experts on nearly every subject involving the running of the beverage operation. They are at the point-of-sale of nearly every transaction. They possess firsthand knowledge on how the clientele reacts to your operation's prices, products and promotions, and know how they compare with your direct competitors'. Soliciting their feedback on relevant matters will help create a sense of involvement among the staff while tapping into their cumulative experience and knowledge.

- **Manage by Example** — Employees are not managed. Figures and objects are managed, people are led. Managing by example is an essential form of leadership. A manager who voluntarily gets behind the bar during a frantically busy shift is an illustration of an individual managing by example. Leadership is a dynamic and effective means of creating a stable, positive working environment.

- **Help Your Bartenders Earn More Money** — It is clearly in your best interest to ensure your bartenders are earning a livable income. The more money your staff is capable of earning the less reason there will be to leave. In addition, the more money your bartenders are earning, the less likely it is that they will risk stealing from the bar. Management can play an active role in helping the bartending staff earn more by ensuring that servers and cocktail servers tip-out to the bar and the bar receives an equitable share of the gratuities earned on transfers to the dining room. A portion of a bartending meeting could be allocated to exchanging ideas on how to increase tips.

- **Make It Easier for Bartenders to Work Efficiently** — It is in your best interest to remove any unnecessary impediments preventing your bartenders from carrying out their job description. For example, bartenders are often required to provide beverage service to patrons seated at the cocktail tables. When business is brisk, it is extremely difficult to wait on customers at the bar, fill drink orders for servers and still provide competent service to patrons seated in the lounge. The more difficult it is for the staff to perform their assigned duties the more hassled they'll be and the more likely they will fall victim to "job burnout."

- **Provide Bartenders with Benefits** — Periodic pay raises are not always feasible, nor the most cost-effective method of providing them with more financial incentive. There are numerous employee benefits which are both affordable and well-received, such as day-care or transportation reimbursement, pre- or post-shift meals, dental or health insurance, and profit sharing. You could encourage and financially compensate your employees to continue their education. It is an excellent means of generating good will, while at the same time creating personal stability within your staff.

- **Provide Staff with the Necessary Support** — It is important for the staff to know that you will provide them with immediate support and backing when dealing with the drinking public. In situations where the bartender is forced to refuse further service of alcohol to a patron, it makes it easier to exercise that right when your bartenders know they have your full support and assistance. It is crucial that the refusal be handled correctly. It is also important that employees maintain their trust in management.

MISMANAGEMENT OF EMPLOYEES AND ITS AFFECT ON INTERNAL THEFT

It is important to identify that management can positively and negatively affect the attitude and morale of the personnel. Quite often, the ability and character of the management staff to create a positive working environment can have a significant impact on the incidence of internal theft, as well as on-the-job substance abuse and absenteeism.

Human nature dictates that if a manager treats his or her employees with respect the staff will respond in kind. It also stands to reason that if one individual can manage to bring out the best in a group, another individual could mismanage the same group of people, negatively affecting their attitude, morale and performance.

Mismanagement practices can be defined as managerial actions that could be defined as unfair, arbitrary, irrational or biased. They combine to create a strained, stressful working environment that will adversely affect productivity and cost control efforts.

A food and beverage operation can be an extremely stressful place to earn a living. Working under pressure, there are a number of ways that a manager can negatively affect morale and productivity. The following items detail fifteen commonly observed mismanagement practices, look at why they are considered counterproductive and how they can be avoided.

- **Verbal Reprimands** — Verbally reprimanding an employee in front of fellow employees or customers, is not only embarrassing for everyone involved, it can also drive a wedge between the staff and management, creating an "us against them" attitude. The appropriate time and place to reprimand or discipline an employee is after the person's shift in the privacy of the office. This will spare the employee humiliation and from having to work the shift with the burden of a reprimand. Naturally, ensuring that the basis for the warning is valid is of primary importance.

- **Misrepresentation** — Initially overselling an employee on the company and the person's role in the future of the business is ill-advised. It is human nature for an employee to become disillusioned and resentful when reality sets in and the person sees the job or company for what it really is. The business is best served by giving a prospective employee an accurate portrayal of what his or her job will be and what the person can realistically expect to earn. There are serious consequences when employees perceive they have been misled by management regarding issues affecting their livelihood.

- **Lack of Guidance** — Failing to initially provide employees with the company's policies and procedures can create an inequitable situation. The most effective way to get a group of people to achieve a level of competency is to first inform them exactly what is expected of them. If employees are not given definitive guidelines governing their on-the-job performance, management cannot reasonably hold them accountable to professional standards of conduct.

- **Lack of Training** — Failing to furnish the personnel with adequate training and supervision does a disservice to the business and employee alike. The business suffers because the staff will not be nearly as competent and productive as they could be. The employees performance will suffer by comparison and be evaluated without sufficient training, a decided liability. As a result, their ability to earn a decent livelihood is hampered.

- **Obvious Bias** — When a manager demonstrates an obvious bias or preference for certain employees, it inevitably engenders feeling of ill-will among the other members of the staff. It is unreasonable to expect the others on the staff to passively tolerate inconsistent treatment, especially if it affects their ability to make a living. Management's objective should be to create a cohesive, tightly knit staff, not to be divisive.

- **Lack of Maturity** — A manager that exhibits irrational or immature behavior undermines his or her ability to be a strong leader. Included on the list, not limited to, is inappropriate behavior such as being intoxicated at work or making sexual advances toward employees. Respect is a vital aspect of authority.

- **Lack of Feedback** — Failing to periodically evaluate employee attitudes and performance makes it less likely that the staff will achieve their fullest potential. Periodic evaluations afford the personnel the opportunity to learn about the perceived quality of their on-the-job performance. In addition, any deficiencies can be addressed and a plan can be devised to help the employee overcome the problem.

- **Scheduling Inequities** — Few things are more closely associated with an employee's livelihood than the weekly schedule. Unfulfilled scheduling requests, over- or under-scheduling, or preferential treatment towards certain employees can lead to rapid and consistent turnover. Equity, aptitude and experience should be the prescribed criteria behind scheduling.

- **Lack of Support** — Without positive reinforcement, employee enthusiasm, initiative and motivation are difficult to maintain. Failing to reward or acknowledge an employee's on-the-job performance can be a serious error of omission. Encouragement and positive feedback go a long way in helping employees reach their fullest potential.

- **Admitting Fallibility** — Respect and admiration can be won or lost. Managers who cannot bring themselves to admit that he or she has made a mistake to an employee damages their authority and ability to lead. Perfection is an impossible standard to attempt to maintain.

- **Lack of Motivation** — Any food and beverage operation requires a motivated and well-trained staff in order to continue to grow as a business. One of the most significant reasons for employees to leave a business is lack of advancement and infrequent wage increases. For individuals to remain motivated and enthusiastic they must be challenged and continually prompted to mature professionally. It is a mistake to expect employees to remain inspired and conscientious without management's assistance.

- **Lack of Tipped Income** — It is definitely in management's best interest to ensure that their employees are more than adequately compensated for their efforts. Therefore, any managerial decision or policy that hinders the employees ability to earn a reasonable tipped income may be interpreted by the staff as managerial disregard and foster discontent.

- **Lack of Credibility** — When management fails to follow through on stated policy decisions or to rectify problem situations it undermines management's credibility. It also sends a negative message to the staff that they cannot necessarily trust what management says it is going to do.

- **Inconsistent Behavior** — Failing to discipline employees for infractions of policies and procedures, and permitting mediocre on-the-job performance negatively affects staff attitude and morale. Why should employees make a concerted effort to follow the establishment's policies if there are no consequences associated with breaking them? Likewise, if mediocrity is tolerated and some employees' abilities are allowed to remain barely adequate, the entire staff will suffer by association and the operation's professionalism as a whole will be diminished.

- **Social Involvement** — Becoming socially involved with the staff causes needless entanglements and seriously hampers management's ability to lead effectively. While a warm, congenial relationship between the staff and management should be fostered, outside fraternization or sexual involvement is detrimental to the operation.

SUBSTANCE ABUSE AND
ITS AFFECT ON INTERNAL THEFT

On-the-job substance abuse is a very real, serious operational problem, one which especially plagues bars and restaurants. Employees who take illegal drugs prior to, or during their shift, exhibit the disregard necessary to steal from one's employer. If your employees are using illegal drugs at work, there exists an extremely strong possibility they are also stealing. Experience and observation dictate that trouble travels in pairs.

THE LEGAL ASPECTS OF EMPLOYEE DISENGAGEMENT

In this litigious society, you must exercise extreme caution when firing an employee. It's unfortunate, but true, the art of disengagement has become an invaluable managerial faculty to possess. As a result, if you strongly suspect an employee of stealing from the your business, there are several important guidelines to consider when firing the person for internal theft.

- **A** — If you fire an employee and cite internal theft as the reason, you better be fully prepared to prove it in a court of law or in front of the National Labor Relations Board. There is nothing which compels ownership to declare internal theft as the cause for termination.

- **B** — When an employee is fired, two managers should be present during the meeting. It may be necessary at a later date for one of the managers to confirm the legitimacy and propriety of the other manager's handling of the situation. The employee may be dissuaded from making false allegations surrounding the circumstances of the termination.

  In addition, the manager conducting the employee's formal discharge should record the precise nature of the discharge on the establishment's termination notice form. The document should contain: the person's name; job title; a clearly worded reason for the firing; and an effective date. All parties should sign the document. If the employee refuses to sign the notice, the witness should make note of that fact on the notice.

- **C** — Even after an employee is terminated, management must exercise restraint regarding the true nature of the dismissal. If the former employee uses the ownership as a reference and a potential employer calls seeking a recommendation, the safest course of action is to give the caller oblique answers, using a strategy of neither confirming or denying any and all inquiries. It might not be the most forthright approach, but it is the most legally cautious approach. The legal pitfall with reference calls is inadvertently saying something which could be construed as defamation of the former employee's character, serving as grounds for a charge of deprivation of livelihood.

For more information on controlling costs and increasing profitability visit www.BarMedia.com